FARMERS AND NOBLES

The Genealogy History of Two Italian American Families

By

Robert Sorrentino

Published by:

Janaway Publishing, Inc.
732 Kelsey Ct.
Santa Maria, California 93454
(805) 925-1952
www.janawaygenealogy.com

2022

Front Cover: Ruffo Castle in Scilla Calabria,
                Photo by Robert Sorrentino
                Farmland is near Capracotta Molise,
                Photo by Nicole Sorrentino

Back Cover: Front and back postcard from Author's
                Grandmother to Great Grandfather:

                *Translation: To my dear dad to always
                remind him of his dear daughter.*

ISBN: 978-1-59641-470-9

Dedication

I thought a lot about who I should dedicate this book to and decided the most appropriate people would be my four Italian grandparents, Ubaldo Sorrentino, Luisa Piromallo, Luigi Nicoletti, and Marietta Nicoletti.

I do not know why they came to America, but like most Italian immigrants, they adopted and loved their new home, while never forgetting where they came from. They instilled the love of family in their children and grandchildren and passed on Italian traditions. I believe that we are who we are because of them.

Marietta and Luigi Nicoletti

Ubaldo Sorrentino and Luisa Piromallo

Special thanks to my wife Marian, who has supported my family research, blog and the creation of this book.

Preface

When I was growing up, I always loved going through the photo album with my mom. Back in those days, we had books with a wooden cover, with the black pages and little pasted corners to hold the photos. I would ask mom who the people were and what their relation was to us. One thing that always stood out was a card the said Nicola Piromallo "dei duchi diCapracotta." Mom would tell me that Nicola was my paternal great-grandfather, or my father's maternal grandfather. She would tell me that he was a duke or a count in Italy. I was always fascinated by this, but never really asked a lot of questions. Many years later, I began my research of my ancestors with Nicola Piromallo's card.

Calling Card of Nicola Piromallo

I did not set my research goals very high. In the beginning, I thought I might find something interesting about Nicola Piromallo and go back a few generations. On my mom's side, knowing that they were farmers, I expected to find out who my great-grandparents were, or maybe go back one more generation after that. I never thought that my research would lead me to create a blog, record audio and video podcasts, and write a book.

Most of us who research our family history believe there is some external force driving us to discover our genealogy. In fact, many people who I have interviewed have told me that they believe we are chosen by our ancestors to tell their story. During my interviews, I have heard some very interesting and compelling stories about how they found a piece of documentation or met living relatives whom they had never known. Later in the book I will reveal some of these stories. Some are so intriguing that you cannot just call it a coincidence.

My goal is to share my family research and inspire people to start or continue their own research. I truly believe there is a "spiritual guidance" bestowed on some of us; we just need hear the voice.

Table of Contents

The Calling

I have interviewed over sixty people and probably had some sort of contact with well over a hundred, and everyone says the same thing: that they are driven to find answers from the past.

Some of the stories are just unbelievable! My own personal story is as follows:

For many years I was researching my dad's two families, Piromallo and Sorrentino. I was pretty sure that my dad's mom was from the Piromallo Capece Piscicelli line that I found, but I wanted to be 100 percent positive. Sorrentino, on the other hand, was a complete roadblock. I hired a professional genealogist in Italy to help me get past these blocks. Bella Italia Genealogy came back quickly with records for Piromallo and confirmed not only my research, but that the people I found in Italy were indeed cousins. For almost a year I was waiting for some clues on the Sorrentino family, and I had pretty much given up any hope that they would produce any records. My go-to person for both families was my cousin, Luisa De Maria. Her mom was my dad's older sister, and they had lived with my grandparents. One day, I got the sad news that Luisa passed away. Two days later, I received a dump of Sorrentino records from Bella Italia. Coincidence? Maybe, but there are so many stories that are just too strange to discount.

One story was told to me by Traci Callister who wanted to find her family from a small village in northern Italy. She befriended a person on Facebook who lived near the village and offered to help. During the trip planning, she narrowed down her bed & breakfast choices to two. She used the "eenie, meeny, miny, moe" method to make her section and phoned Italy. As she was booking the place, the person on the other end inquired why she wanted to be in such a small town. She told her that her great-grandmother had lived there, and she was searching for her roots. She went on to say that her grandmother had no heirs and left her property to another family in the town. The woman on the phone said, "Hold on, I have to get my mother." As it turned out, this was the family that her grandmother had willed the property to.

Another story was told to me by Paul Nautua, from familysearch.org. Paul was going to a conference in Pennsylvania and knew that his grandmother was married in Hoboken, New Jersey. He had hit a major roadblock with her. Shortly before the trip, he asked her out loud, "Grandma, give me a clue." He was in the booth at the conference, when he saw a woman with a name tag that said she was from the NJ State Archives. He approached her and told her about his roadblock, not expecting anything. The next day, the woman came up to him just before his presentation and gave him an envelope and told him to open it after his talk. He said that he could barely get through his presentation and once finished, he immediately opened the envelope. Much to his surprise and delight, it was his grandmother's birth record!

I often find that I may be researching one person only to come across something totally unrelated that will bring me to another person. Sometimes something just pops into my head; I enter some crazy search on Google and find something that has eluded me for years.

It's also amazing to me how most of us who have been doing this research have a deep attachment to Italy when we are in the country. It feels like home and it's as if some force wants you there. Why is it that some people have this urgency to find these records? I cannot stress enough to people who are just starting out, to try every kind of wild search on names, places, and even occupations. We are blessed in this age that we can do a lot of research from our homes. I'm always poking around, trying different combinations of names and places, with hopes of finding an ancestor or record that I have not yet come across.

My friend Alessandro Bovino from Bella Italia Genealogy told me the following story:

> We were walking down the street in a small town where I brought one of my clients to find his roots, when an old woman asked who we are and what we were doing. I explained my client's story and she pulled out a huge key and took us to a little chapel dedicated to St. Lucy, the patron of eyesight. At the bottom of her statue were various objects and medals from people petitioning her for intercession. The tradition is to pick up a piece and hold it to your eyes and have a photo taken. Bob, my client, picked up one piece only, and held it to his eyes and shouted, "What's going on?" You won't believe this. The piece

he picked up had the names of his great great-grandparents from over one hundred years ago.

Another story from, Steve Williams, one of my interviewees was when he went into a small town in Campania called Tuoro. His cousin wanted him to visit the church in the town and he convinced the priest to let them in to look for records. Here is his story:

> The church was over one thousand years old and looking at the walls of the church there were all names that I recognized from my research. As I was sitting there, I looked up and saw an inlaid crucifix. It was an exact match for a crucifix I had bought years before a hundred miles away. When I explained to the priest, he said, "Of course, who do you think brought you here? God did and he's giving you a sign."

One final story from Michael Fattorosi is amazing and illustrates how you can find the most incredible things if you go with your instinct. Michael did not know much about his family, and more or less assumed they were just regular people. When his father passed, he asked his

The author in Sorrento 1996

great-uncle if he knew anything about the family. His uncle told him that he didn't know much, other than he thought they were fairly well-off, and were from a town called Gragnano in Campania. Michael noted it and forgot about it.

Many years later, while in Positano and with the rain pouring down, he picked up the tourist magazine in the hotel and saw that he was very close to Gragnano. The next day he hired a driver to take him and his wife to see if he could find any records. On their way the driver asked, "Why do you want to go to Gragnano?"

Michael responded, "To find ancestors."

The driver told him that he should go to Lettere, as there are more records there. Michael explained to me that normally he would have said no, as he doesn't like to change plans. When they arrived at the town hall, his driver explained to the clerk who Michael was and told them to go to the church across the way as they would have more records. Michael found out that not only was his family from Lettere, but they went back a thousand years and had some nobility status. Not only that, but he was also able to find documents written by one of his ancestors!

Sorrentino

I could never figure out why my grandparents, Ubaldo Sorrentino and Luisa Piromallo, came to the United States. My dad never mentioned it, and I never asked, so it is quite possible that he did not know. I do know that my grandfather came about a year before my grandmother, and at some point, he opened an embroidery business with his brother, Riccardo. I always assumed that my grandmother did not have any relatives in the US, until I discovered that a Maria Piromallo and her husband, Tomasso Pergamo, came to New York City in 1905. It took a very long time, but eventually I ascertained that Maria was my great-grandaunt. I can only assume that Maria communicated to my grandparents and persuaded them to come to the United States. I learned later that Tomasso was an entrepreneur and had either a shoe or wallet business, so maybe he was looking for help running the business. It's also possible that he bankrolled Ubaldo to start his business. In the 1940's and 1950's, Ubaldo and Riccardo employed Tomasso's descendants.

Arrival of Luigia Piromallo and children Achille, Emilia and Maria

1915 Census showing the family in NYC

Sorrentino Shop c. 1918

Sorrentino Family c 1920

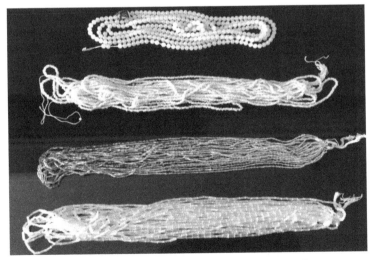

Beads from the Sorrentino Embroidery Shop

At some point during my research, I began to question my cousin Paul about this relationship. Initially, he was not sure, until I gave him an address. That address was 419 E 15th St, and he was shocked! He said, "Repeat that for me?"

So I did.

He said, "That's where my mother fell out the window."

For context, my aunt fell out of the fifth-floor window when she was about five years old. Apparently, like most tenement buildings in NYC at the time, clothes lines were strung across the courtyard between the buildings. These clothes lines broke the fall and because of them, Aunt Emily came away with just a broken foot.

After we figured all of this out, I started throwing out some more names and locations to Paul, and he remembered all these families from the past. One family that was especially interesting was the Petix family from Queens, NY. Growing up, my dad and mom would tell us that they were going over to see Pete Petix and Aunt Beatrice. Aunt Beatrice was the granddaughter of Maria Piromallo, making her a second cousin of my dad, but- you know Italian Families- as a sign of respect she was called Aunt Beatrice. What makes this so interesting is that about ten years into my research, and maybe five years after discovering Maria Piromallo, I got a message on Ancestry.com from my cousin Linda Sarandrea. We had never met before, at least not that we remember, and she said, "I think we are researching the same person."

"We are," I said.

I went on to tell Linda that Maria was my great-grandfather's sister.

"Are you sure?" she said.

"Absolutely," I replied

In any event, she was not. So, I told her to take an Ancestry test to confirm it, but I was 100 percent positive. A few months later she messaged me, "We're not a match".

How could that be? I thought. I checked and we were. Linda contacted Ancestry and they claimed they made a mistake, and then proceeded to correct it.

But the story does not stop there. In fact, this was just the beginning of how our families were so intertwined between the 1920's and the

1970's. Linda began to go through her grandmother's things and found photos of my dad's family from the 1930's. She had amazing photos of the entire family, including my aunt's weddings and my cousins. My dad's sister, Julia, was very good friends with Aunt Beatrice, and there are several photos of them together. The more we talked, the more things came together. Early on, Paul mentioned the Muesberger family. It was interesting at the time, but I never thought much of it. Well, Aunt Beatrice's daughter, Josephine, married Charles Muesberger, and Josephine's family lived in the same house with her mom and dad. Josephine was best friends with my cousin, Nancy, who was in Josephine's bridal party. Not only that, but Josephine worked in my grandfather's shop and had her bridal veil made by him. Also, I am pretty sure that my dad took her wedding photos!

Bob Sorrentino and Linda Sarandrea

Gene, Linda, Paul, and my sister all finally got to meet at my house, and we had a lot of fun. Gene brought his mom's veil, and Linda brought us all beads from my grandfather's shop that Aunt Beatrice had saved. Paul was able to give us a rundown of the family back then and it was as if we were never separated.

One other final note: In 1972, I moved to an apartment about five blocks away from Aunt Beatrice and Gene's family. I vaguely remember passing by their house and my dad saying that Aunt Beatrice lived there. The apartment I moved to was vacated by my cousin Louise (Nancy and Paul's sister). When I told Gene about this, he said, "the one with the very long staircase? I was there many times."

As I said, Dad's family originally lived in NYC. At some point between 1915 and 1922, they moved to Scotch Plains, NJ. I am not sure why, but I can only surmise that it was because some of Maria Piromallo's family lived in New Jersey, and they liked the area. Apparently, they were fairly well-off because they owned their own home, had a car, and appeared on the society page in the local paper on a regular basis. My Uncle Achille, who was about seventeen years older than my father, met his wife there in the early 1920's. They lived there until about 1930. From what I can piece together, some sort of business deal went bad around that time, or maybe there were issues revolving around the stock market crash. In any event, they moved from New Jersey to Corona, Queens sometime in the 1930's. In the 1940's, most of the brothers and sisters moved to Whitestone, Queens.

Achille, Emily, and Mary, three of dad's older siblings, were born in Cercola, Italy. I never met my grandfather, as he passed away only a couple of months after I was born. I don't remember my Uncle Achille, as he passed away in 1954. My dad's oldest sister, Emily, and her husband, Costanzo, were my godparents. They were wonderful people, and they lived in a two-family home with my grandparents on a very nice block in Whitestone. They had a huge basement, which was sectioned off, and had a big room for family gatherings, a photography darkroom, and another room with Uncle Connie's train layout.

Achille Sorrentino with his godparents

Costanzo and Emily De Maria

I loved going over there. I got to play with the trains as much as I wanted to and would usually spend a week there during the summer. Aunt Emily had blueberry bushes where we would pick the fruit for her pancakes. Uncle Connie would always call me his "Goomba" and had me drinking espresso when I was about seven, much to Mom's dismay. My cousin, Louise, was about five years older than me and we would take the 7 subway train to her piano teacher in Corona. I always had to be in the front car so I could look out the window and watch the tracks. We were probably thirteen and eight at the time. In fact, my cousin Paul said he would make that trip at about twelve years old to bring my grandfather's embroidery work to Manhattan! Things have certainly changed.

We had great Christmas events there and would exchange gifts by the fireplace, then go down to the basement to have a big meal. Back then it was not unusual for the kids to get a glass of wine tempered with water. After the meal, my uncles would play cards and I remember Uncle Connie letting me sweep the table and stack his coins when he won.

Uncle Connie was born on the Isle of Capri and came to the United States when he was only sixteen. Through family research, I found that his grandfather, Maggiore Giuseppe De Maria, was once governor of the isle. Uncle Connie was a big man, much bigger than the Sorrentino's for sure, and worked in the restaurant business in NYC for many years. Eventually he became the Maître d'hôtel for the exclusive Century Club.

Aunt Mary and Uncle Tommy were great people who lived only a few blocks from Aunt Emily and Uncle Connie. During a very long six-month newspaper strike, my aunt left a box of food for my dad to pick up. I don't think we really needed it all that much, but it was a nice gesture on their part. They had a beautiful house with a very large backyard and an above ground pool, where they would invite the nieces and nephews over for a swim.

My dad was a photographer for the NY Daily News. Separately, he would also take wedding photos on the weekends. The darkroom was his domain, and I would go with him on Saturdays and watch him develop the wedding photos. It was quite a process in the 1950's and early 1960's. My dad used a Speed Graphic camera, which had a plate that allowed for two shots. After the first shot you would reverse the plate and take the second shot. Additionally, you had to change the flashbulb after every shot. Whether he was working for the paper, or doing wedding photos, Dad always had to carry around a large bag with plates and flash bulbs.

Dad (first on the right) on the job

Aunt Julia and Uncle Anthony were also wonderful people. Aunt Julia was a sewing teacher for Singer Sewing machines and an incredible seamstress. She would make clothes for my sister's Barbie dolls. Quite remarkable! I just recently learned that she went to the Fashion Institute of Technology in NYC and designed dresses back in the 1930's. I don't know for sure, but I would guess that she also worked in my grandfather's business when she was young.

Aunt Julia with designer dress

For the longest time, I was not able to find any records on the Sorrentino family in Italy. Bella Italia Genealogy did a great job for me and found records for the Sorrentino family going back several generations.

Surprisingly, I have been able to trace my 2nd great-grandmother Maria Michela Longo back to her maternal great-grandparents, Isai Priscolo and Orsala Cennamo. Their daughter, Mariangela Priscolo (1737-1811), married Pasquale Scafura. Their daughter, Eleonora Scarfura (1769-1844), married Paolo Longo.

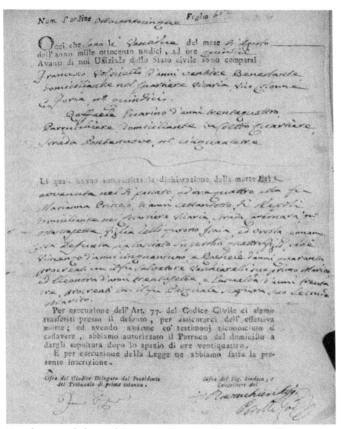

On the 22nd day of August 1815, Raffaele Guarino, age 34 testified to the death of Marianna Priscolo, age 78, living in the Vicaria district 87 Carbonara street. She was the daughter of Isai Priscolo and Orsala Cemmano. First married to Salvatore Vecharelli and second to Pasquale Scarfuro

L'anno mille ottocento quarantaquattro il dì *Dodici* del mese

di *novembre* alle ore *tredici*

Avanti di Noi *Cavalier Giovan Battista Affatati Aggiunto*

ed Ufiziale dello Stato Civile del Circondario *Vicaria*

Comune di Napoli, Provincia di Napoli, sono comparsi *Rafaelle Baldino*

di *Napoli*

di anni *ventisei* di professione *scrivente*

domiciliato *Palazzo due Porte a Caperti*

numero tre

e *Francesco di Maria* di *Napoli*

di anni *quarantasei* di professione *scrivente*

domiciliato *vico Gigante numero quindici*

I quali han dichiarato, che nel giorno *undici del*

del mese *di* anno *corrente* alle

ore *ventiquattro* è mort *nella sua casa* *Eleonora*

Scafura

di *Napoli* di anni *settantanove*

di professione

domiciliato *vico Longo a Carbonara numero centonove*

figlio *di furono Pasquale proprietario, e di Mariangela*

Priscolo, vedova di Paolo Longo, scrivente, avendo rima-

sto due figli di età maggiore

Per esecuzione della legge, ci siamo trasferiti, insieme co' detti Testimonj, presso la persona defunta, e ne abbiamo riconosciuta la sua ef-
fettiva morte. Abbiamo indi formato il presente Atto, che abbiamo inscritto sopra i due registri, e datane lettura a' dichiaranti, si è nel giorno, mese, ed anno, come sopra, segnato da Noi.

Rafaele Baldino

On the 12th of November 1844 Rafaelle Baldino age 26 a writer living
at 3 Palazzo due Porte and Caperti and Francesco Di Maria age 46 a
writer living at 15 Vico Gigante testified to the death of Eleonora Scafura age 79 living at 25 Vico Longo a Carbonara

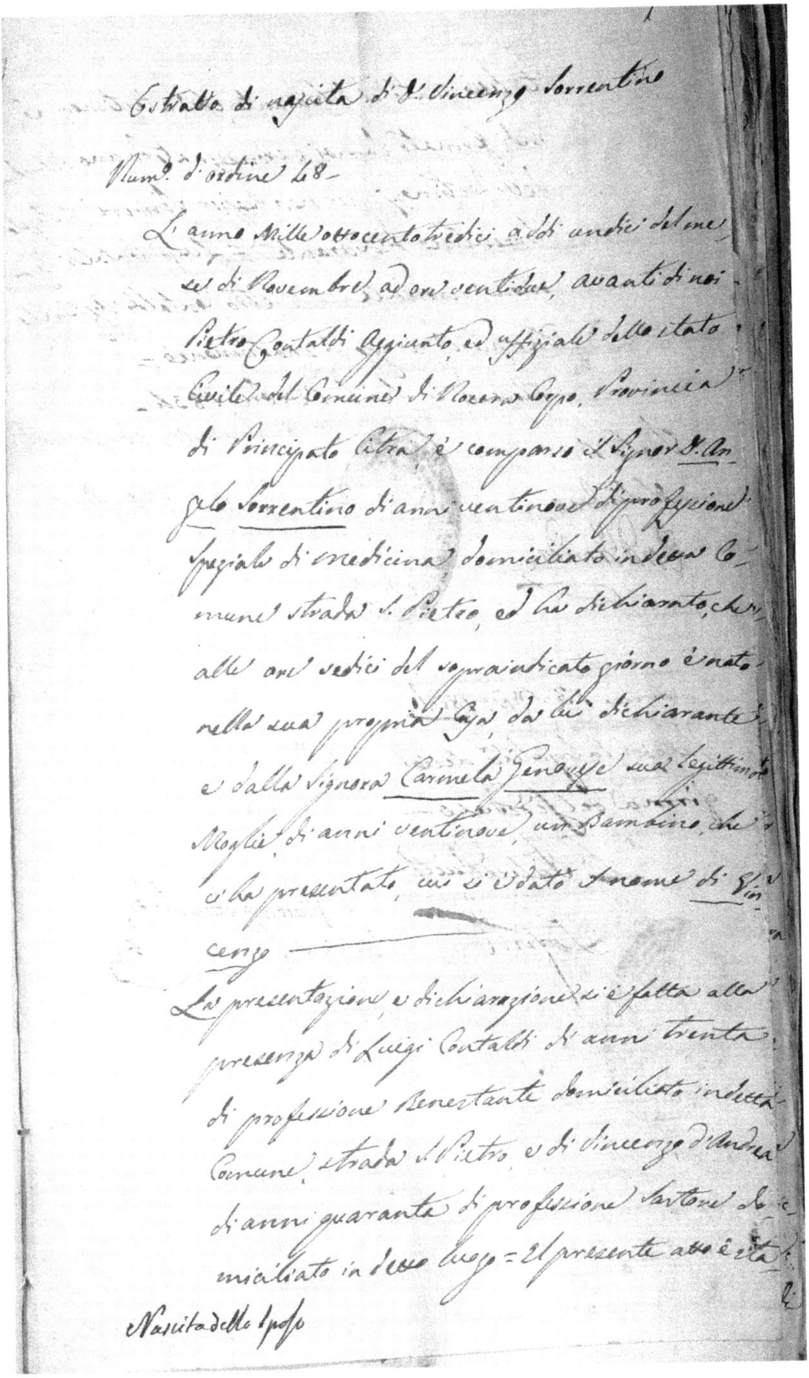

Estratto di nascita di D. Vincenzo Sorrentino

Num.º d'ordine 68 —

L'anno Mille ottocento tredici, addì undici del mese
se di Novembre, ad ore ventidue, avanti di noi
Pietro Contaldi Aggiunto, ed uffiziale dello stato
Civile del Comune di Nocera Corpo, Provincia
di Principato Citra, è comparso il Signor D. Angelo Sorrentino di anni ventinove di professione
Speziale di medicina domiciliato in detto Comune strada S. Pietro, il ha dichiarato, che,
alle ore sedici del sopraindicato giorno è nato,
nella sua propria Casa, da lui dichiarante
e dalla Signora Carmela Genovese sua legittima
Moglie, di anni ventinove, un Bambino, che
si ha presentato, cui si è dato il nome di Vincenzo —

La presentazione, e dichiarazione si è fatta alla
presenza di Luigi Contaldi di anni trenta
di professione Benestante domiciliato in detto
Comune, strada S. Pietro, e di Vincenzo d'Andrea
di anni quaranta di professione Sartore domiciliato in detto luogo = Il presente atto è sta

Nascita dello Sposo

[17]

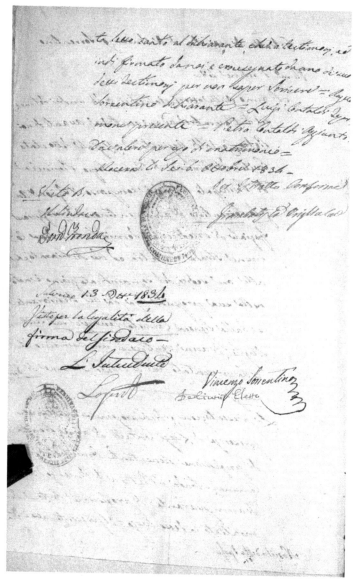

On 22 November 1813 Angelo Sorrentino age 29 living at Strada de San Pietro presented a male baby from his legitimate wife Carmela Genovese, witnessed by Luigi Contaldi age 30 a rich person and Vincenzo D'Andrea age 40. The child's name Vincenzo.

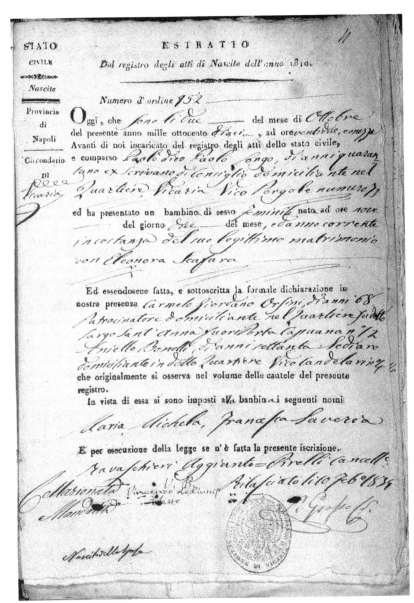

On the 12th day of October 1810 Paulo Longo age 41 lawyer and counsel and living in the Vicaria district of 73 Vico Pergola presented a female baby from his legitimate wife Eleonora Scafura witnessed by Carmelo Giordano Orsini age 68 and Aniello Bonelli age 70. Looks like they were both domestics the baby's name is Maria Michela Francesca Saveria

In 1834, Vincenzo Sorrentino, my second great-grandfather, married Maria Michela Longo, and they had quite a lengthy marriage contract. I believe because her father was a lawyer. I won't publish the entire record, but here is the gist of what it says:

Before us, notary Agostino Primicerio of the late Giuseppe, residing in the hamlet of Portaromana in this municipality of Nocera, and [before] the undersigned witnesses to us known, according to the Law, personally appeared Don Angelo Sorrentino of the late don Tomasso, pharmacist aged 50, and Donna Carmela Genovese of the late Vincenzo, aged 47, spouses well known to us, residing in this municipality of Nocera, and in the San Pietro hamlet, who with this present act give and concede their full consent to their son Don Vincenzo Sorrentino, attorney at law aged 22, residing in Napoli, Vico Longo a Carbonara number 40, as to enter into a true and lawful marriage with Donna Maria Michela Francesca Saveria Longo, daughter of Don Paolo and of Donna

Eleonora Scafuro, unmarried aged 25, residing with her father in Napoli in the said Vico Longo a Carbonara number 40, and this according to the prescriptions of the civil and canonical laws, also declaring that this son of theirs is unmarried, never belonged, nor belongs, to any troop, either of land or the sea, nor was enrolled in the army, having always practiced as a lawyer, and never was employed in the ministry of war, and finally never received any veteran pension.

Because of the foregoing, this act has been drafted and read to the appearing spouses, and to the witnesses, and they all declared that it was by them well understood.

Done, read, and published by us the above said notary and in our studio located in the above mentioned Portaromana hamlet of the above said municipality of Nocera, province of Principato Citeriore, and before the above said spouses, and [before] the below said witnesses messers. don Ignazio Lamberti of the living Pasquale, owner residing in the said San Pietro hamlet, and Domenico Carpentiere of the late Pasquale, owner residing in the said Portaromana hamlet, both of this municipality, having the qualities required by the laws, who declare that they know the above said appearers, and together with them they have signed [this act], except for Donna Carmela Genovese who has declared before us and the witnesses that she is not able to write.

I think what is very interesting is the bit about never being in the ministry of war and never receiving a military pension.

Vincenzo Sorrentino and Maria Michela had four children that I have found. Maria Cristina, 1838, Emilia Elisabetta, 1840, Achille, 1842, and Maria Carmela, 1845.

Achille Sorrentino married Giulia Domenica Princi, and they had six children, however I have only been able to find four to date. Ubaldo (1883–1951), Carlo Ugo (b 1885), Riccardo (1888-1985), and Pia (b 1888). Ubaldo and Riccardo came to the United States, and Pia later became Sister Alfonsina, and was a nun in Salerno for over sixty years.

La presentazione, e dichiarazione anzidetta si è fatta alla presenza di Don *[handwritten]* di *[handwritten]* di anni *[handwritten]* di professione *[handwritten]* domiciliato *[handwritten]*

e di *[handwritten]* di *[handwritten]* di anni *[handwritten]* di professione *[handwritten]* domiciliato *[handwritten]*

Testimonj intervenuti al presente Atto, e dal Dichiarante prodotti.

Il presente Atto, che abbiamo all' uopo formato, è stato inscritto ne' due registri, letto al Dichiarante, ed a' Testimonj; ed indi nel giorno, mese; ed anno, come sopra, firmato da Noi. *[handwritten]*

On 13 December 1842 Vincenzo Sorrentino age 28 and living at 28 Vico Longo in Naples presented a male named a Achille Maria Luccio Aniello from his legitimate wife Maria Michela Longo witnessed by Don Giuseppe Contrafano a Doctor of Letters living at 78 Vico Longo Carbonaro and Francesca Di Maria a servant living at 15 Vico Gigante.

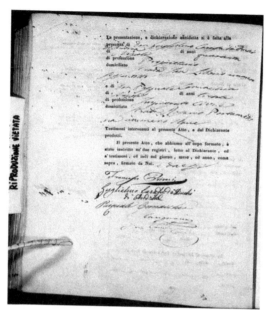

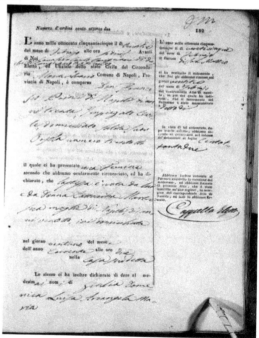

On 21 February 1855 Don Francesco Princi age 30, a civil clerk presented a female baby from his legitimate wife Donna Caterina Matre age 28. Born on the 21st of this month named Giulia Arcangela Maria baptized on 25 February at San Matteo.

Pia Sorrentino (Sister Alfonsina)

One thing about research is that you sometimes find things in the most unlikely places. I was able to find some interesting facts about Italy from a local New Jersey newspaper. For example, no one knew that my great- grandfather, Achille Sorrentino, was a Supreme Court justice in Naples. Both are from the 1920's:

Local News Notes

Ubaldo Sorrentino, of Farley avenue, has received word from Italy of the death of his mother, Marchesa Giulda Princi Sorrentino, who was the widow of the late Justice of the Supreme Court of Naples, Marchese Achille Sorrentino. There are three sons and three daughters surviving. Two sons resided in this country. They are: Richard Sorrentino, of Brooklyn, and Ubaldo Sorrentino, of Scotch Plains.

The Teen Age Group of the Methodist Episcopal Church will

Obituary of my great-grandmother Giulia Princi

Mr. and Mrs. Clarence Sharkey, has returned home from Sunnyside, where she spent some time recuperating after an operation performed at Muhlenberg Hospita six weeks ago.

Mr. and Mrs. Ubaldo Sorrentino of Farley avenue, have received news from Italy of the death of their uncle, Count Luigi Caracciolo, prince of Torchiarolo. He leaves hi swife, one son and two sisters.

Horace Hatfield, son of Mr. and Mrs. John Z. Hatfield, who is a student at Rutgers' University, spent the week-end with his parents.

Mrs. Robert Tichenor, of West-

Obituary of my grandmother's uncle

Two more announcements from the 1920's

Engagement Announced

Mrs. Pierre H. Moore of 407 East Seventh street gave a birthday party New Year's Eve in honor of her daughter, Claire Frances Morris, whose engagement to Archille M. E. Sorrentino, son of Mr. and Mrs. Ubaldo Sorrentino of Scotch Plains, was announced.

The evening was spent in games. Refreshments were served at midnight, when Nicholas Victor Sorrentino, attired in New Year's costume, brought greetings to all.

Engagement of my Uncle Achille

Julia Sorrentino Tendered Party

Julia Sorrentino, the daughter of Mr. and Mrs. Ubaldo Sorrentino, of Farley avenue, was yesterday tendered a party at her home in honor of her ninth birthday by her sister, Emily. Twelve guests were present.

A delightful afternoon was spent in a program of games. The little hostess was the recipient of many beautiful gifts. A surprise birthday cake, the gift of Mr. and Mrs. Pierre Moore, delighted the guests. The home was attractively decorated in a color scheme of pink and white.

Aunt Julia's birthday 1925

[27]

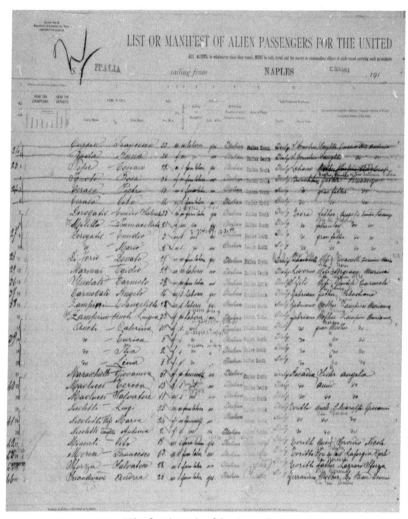

Nicoletti arrival in America

Nicoletti

I never thought I would be able to trace the Nicoletti family back as far as I did. I did not know my great-grandparent's names and could not find the death records of them online. One day, I mentioned this to my mom, and she told me that she had the records. With that information, I started to research the Antenati. Surprisingly, Bari has most of its records online and indexed. I found that my grandmother was from Toritto, and my grandfather was from Acquaviva Della Fonte. Interestingly enough, both my grandparents were Nicoletti's but not related. Supposedly the name comes from a group of men who went to Turkey to confiscate the relics of St. Nicholas of Myra in Turkey in 1087.

My Nicoletti grandparents married in Toritto Bari in 1908. From what I was told, they had eleven children, but two died in infancy while they were still in Italy. I was told that they came to the United States in 1915 because WWI had broken out and my grandmother was concerned that my grandfather would be called back into the army. He had served in Libya, and she did not want him leaving for war again. When they came with their oldest daughter, Antonia, they left their son, Giovanni, in the care of his grandparents, Francesco Nicoletti and Maria Carnevale.

Some of my fondest memories are the parties in my grandmother's front yard in Corona, Queens. Ever since I can remember, from about the mid 1950's until 1971, every Nicoletti summer party was held in that yard. Rain or shine, it did not matter; the nine sons and daughters, grandchildren, and great-grandchildren would gather.

My dad worked on Sundays, so if Mom was taking too long, I would walk the five blocks in

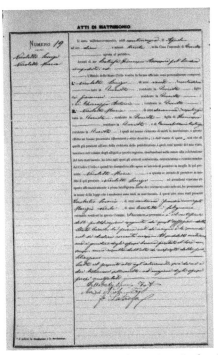

Marriage of Luigi and Maria Nicoletti

College Point to Uncle Tom's and hitch a ride with him. Uncle Tom would let me drive the long stretch along College Point Blvd. to Roosevelt Ave., which was always fun! I loved to be one of the first ones there, but that meant going to Cammeratti's or to the soda warehouse, both about a block away.

Typically, one or more aunts would be in the kitchen making sauce or meatballs, and if you were lucky, you could grab one before it hit the sauce. But more about the food later.

Grandma would get happier as everyone would slowly but surely start to arrive. We would have the aunts and uncles and cousins of course, and then the cousins of cousins, and sometimes the cousins of the cousins of cousins. As we got older, the boyfriends and girlfriends would come too. Pity the non-Italians..., they needed to manage the names and the food. Yes, I will get to the food.

But first, "Go kiss your aunt."

Aunt Mary, Uncle Tony, Aunt Josephine and Grams

Seating was at a premium in grandma's backyard. There was very little around the table under the roof, and that was usually reserved for grandma and grandpa, and the senior aunts and uncles (although, the aunts spent a lot of time in the kitchen). You could then default to the aluminum table(s) set up in the sun (for the older cousins), but you might not be able to squeeze in. Next was the ledge along the grapevines, and finally the ledge leading to the basement stairs (moms did not like that ledge). If you asked where you should sit, Uncle Mike would raise is middle finger and say, "Sit on this."

While the aunts were making the "gravy and gravy meat" (I did say sauce earlier), Uncle Tom was stoking the BBQ. Uncle Tom would start with chicken livers and bacon. I passed on that, then put on the chicken basted with Italian dressing using sprigs of basil as the brush. I'm not a

[30]

fan of lamb, but he would have skewers of lamb that we would squeeze on lemon juice, which was very nice. But the coup de gras, was the Chivalet (thin sausage of lamb, parsley, and cheese). We would line up, Bellacicco's roll in hand, waiting and waiting and waiting. Once you got your sausage, you got back in line with sandwich one to get sandwich two.

Of course, we had some other Nicoletti specialties like Eggplant Parmigiana, Lemon Chicken, and Manicotti. Depending on the occasion, and if we were lucky, there would be Pizza dolce or homemade crumb cake. Visit www.italiangenealogy.blog for the recipes.

Up until the mid-1960's, there was a feast on the block in August during grandma's birthday. Right outside the gate, every year, was the Zeppole stand. Three for a quarter. Other desserts were the fruit and nuts, of course, but we would also get five gallons of Lemon Ice from the Lemon Ice King of Corona. Or sometimes just walk there. And cookies from Mangiapane's.

As I said earlier, for many years the entertainment was the feast right outside grandma's backyard. There were all the typical games, food (not that we needed any), the stage with Italian singers, etc. It was sad when the feast closed.

We also made our own entertainment. One of my older cousins "Lou" decided to knight the younger cousins and give us weird names that we could not remember. He used grandma's cane as the sword and would bop you on the head if you did not remember your name. Did I say this was entertainment!

At some point, Aunt Mary would break into the standard Italian songs, and everyone would join in the singing. UncleTony would play the harmonica or do his Charlie Chaplin imitation. Before he passed away, Uncle Nick Mina would just make everyone crack up. He was one of the funniest guys ever.

But the real fun would start with the kids' "talent contest." We would sing or dance and our uncles would throw change. Zia Rachel would play a fake piano for the dancers and slap her arm (as in "F" you). One time, when my cousin John was dancing, Uncle Mike gave him a quarter and Zia Rachel ten bucks for her piano. That was really a scream.

So sad that these days are gone, but we all have our memories of Grandma's backyard.

Shortly before the NY World's Fair opened in 1964, my Uncle Frank and Aunt Dolly opened Frank's Luncheonette on 108th Street in Corona, Queens. At the time I was thirteen and very excited, as they hired me to work there on weekends and summers while the World's Fair was open.

Uncle Frank

The Fair (as we called it) was only a few blocks away and we would often have tourists and bus drivers come in to eat. In fact, after the fair closed, bus drivers would drive 50 to 60 miles out of their way to dine at Frank's Luncheonette and kibitz with Aunt Dolly. Uncle Frank drove trucks when he was young, and later worked as a baker at Leonard's Up the Station and ran a fish store in the Bronx for several years.

Frank's was a small place with only eight or ten stools and no tables. But we did good business and a lot of take-out. At the front there was a candy and cigarette counter and a place to hold the Daily Papers. Then the lunch counter and soda fountain with a back room with the stove and griddle. We also had the soda cooler that kept the bottles in cold water.

My duties included stocking the candy and cigarettes, putting together the Sunday papers, making fountain sodas and malts (yeah real malts), egg creams (yum), and ice cream sundaes. As time went on, I would make the rice and chocolate pudding. I would also deliver orders to some of the local businesses. However, the very best thing about working at Frank's Luncheonette was the perks. Aunt Dolly was a great cook, as was Uncle Frank. So I had my pick of menu items. My favorite was the eggplant parmigiana or the meatball hero. Uncle Frank would make onions on the grill with a load of butter and paprika that would smother your cheeseburger, always a great choice. On cold days, a nice bowl of chicken soup. Breakfast was a Pechter's corn muffin, buttered and grilled, or one of their cheese danishes. And of course, anything from the fountain, whenever I liked!

I can go on and on about what wonderful people my aunt and uncle were and how it was so great to hang out with them. In the morning, it would just be Uncle Frank and me, and we would talk about the races or sports, make the coffee, put out the danishes, stock the shelves, etc. Did I mention that bus drivers would come miles out of the way to eat and hang out? A lot of it had to do with Aunt Dolly. here are just a few stories:

There used to be a Spanish speaking gentleman who would come in and order bacon and eggs or a hamburger every other day. One day Aunt Dolly asked him, "How come you only order two things?”

His answer was, "Qué?”

When Aunt Dolly realized that he did not speak any English, she told him, "I will give you a different meal every day, and if you like it, I will tell you how to say it in English." Hence, she taught him English.

Aunt Dolly would make some food at home, like frying the chicken or making the eggplant and meatballs. They lived only about three blocks from Frank's Luncheonette, so it was a short walk with the shopping cart.

One day Aunt Dolly came in and dropped the cart in the back for Uncle Frank. He opened it up and yelled out, "Dolly, this is garbage!”

She shot back, "It's the stuff I made!”

He said, "No it's the garbage!”

And it was! In her haste she threw the food away and brought the garbage to the store.

Believe me, we had some great characters. My aunt and uncle rented the place from "Butch", who also happened to be my Aunt Ann's cousin. Butch was a taxi driver, and his home was behind Frank's Luncheonette, with an alley, where Butch would park his car. About once a week, we would hear a loud scraping sound as Butch would get a little too close to the wall of the store.

"Rocky the Barber" (Pal Rocky) would come in for a chat and his Gini Stinkers (di Nobili cigars), quite aptly named.

My cousin's husband, Al, would deliver the bread from Leonard's bakery every day and order a cup of coffee (10 cents) and leave me a 90-cent tip!

Cousin Lou Mina (Mina's Fuel Oil) would come in and say to me, "I'll have a soda.... JERK," and laugh. I later worked for Lou and boy, do I have some stories about that job.

My dad, who worked for the NY Daily News at the time, would come in sometimes and if he ordered a tea, it had to be filled right to the very top of the cup.

After my tenure, my cousin Cathy (Frank and Dolly's daughter) worked there, and my sister Lori too. Eventually Frank's son Lou took over for a while.

Now, there are a lot of Aunt Dolly stories, beginning with the fact that you could never call her by her real first name. Out of respect for her memory, I won't divulge, but she was not very fond of her given name. Aunt Dolly had great energy, and not much seemed to bother her. One time she was baking a cake and she put in the wrong ingredients. No big deal, she just tossed it and started over. She also had a thing about ice- while there was often plenty- it was rationed out carefully.

Her favorite store was John's Bargain Store (for you younger readers, that was the dollar store in the 50's and 60's), and she loved Macy's too, but only the flagship store on Herald Square in NYC.

Since my grandmother lived with Aunt Dolly and Uncle Frank, all the holidays were at their house. The living room was made into a dining room, and we would get twenty to twenty-five in there. We would have the typical all-day feast starting around 1 PM with antipasto, soup, pasta, meat, fruit and nuts, and dessert. What a spread! Christmas Eve was even crazier; there might be fifty people squeezed into the living room and kitchen, with very few seats to be had.

At Christmas my aunts would make homemade manicotti, probably around 100, and I loved them. Aunt Dolly would make her cream cheese cookies filled with jam, which no one can really duplicate. At Easter, Uncle Frank would make homemade ravioli. Watching him was amazing. He would have a big board and a long dowel used as a rolling pin. The pasta would be rolled to a perfect thickness in a minute. With the leftover dough, he would make linguini (grandma called it "lagana" in her Barese dialect). The ravioli would be set out to dry on the sofa for a few hours. One year my cousin Frank sat on the ravioli, which I later wrote a song about.

Aunt Dolly at Frank's

At Christmas, she had the most eclectic nativity scene. You might see two Joseph's, wise men of various sizes and maybe a skier not too far away. She would tell people that my uncle needed a wallet or Old Spice for Christmas, so it was always great fun to see the gifts opened.

Before talking about my two summers working at Mina's, a brief history as I know it: I was told that the company was started by my aunt's father-in-law, I guess in the 30's or 40's. My aunt's husband (Nick Mina) was running the company when I was a boy.

Now Uncle Nick was a card. He used to make me laugh all the time, especially when he would deliver oil to our house in College Point. My mom had a special gold chair in our living room that no one was allowed to sit on. Uncle Nick knew this and whenever Mom would have him come in for coffee, he would go sit on that chair with his oil burner clothes, just to freak her out.

I was about ten when he passed, and we were actually vacationing with him and my aunt. It was so sad, and I remember every detail of that night.

During Easter vacation of 1967, when we were having some snow squalls, my cousin Lou came to deliver our oil. He asked me what I was doing, and I said not much. He asked, "Do you want to work on the truck?"

I said, "You bet!"

So, I ran and got some old clothes and off we went. Little did I know that I was the guy who was going to bring the hose to the house, while Lou sat in the truck. But that was fine, I didn't really mind. It was fun and I made some cash. One of the best parts was climbing to the top of the truck and filling up the three bays with 2,700 gallons of oil.

I guess I did a good job, because once the summer rolled around Lou asked if I would like to help clean the oil burners.

After you ran the cleaning fluid though, you would have to prime the pump on the oil burner. You did this by putting a wrench on the plug and bleeding out the air. One time, I had the wrench on and was holding it to bleed, as Lou threw the switch to start the pump. As soon as he hit the switch, I was getting electrocuted. I kept yelling turn it off, he kept yelling why. Finally, he turned it off. The worst part was that I couldn't let go of the wrench. Another time, after bleeding the pump, the igniter wasn't working, so I opened the door to the chamber and BOOM, it ignited. Knocked me clear across the floor.

One of the accounts was a funeral home. We had to go deep into the basement past all the embalming rooms. We brought everything in, and Lou said, "I'll be right back," and as he walked out, he was shutting all the lights going, "oooooh oooooh."

When he came back, I said, "I couldn't see."

Lou then said, "Why didn't you just walk around and feel for the light switch, or an arm or leg?"

One of the funniest events was at Future Motors in Long Island City. They a had a very large underground tank, which held probably 1,000 gallons. The fill was basically just a hole in the ground with no vent, and the nozzle didn't lock in. So, as I'm watching the nozzle, the hose starts to bounce. Thinking it was going to pop out I went to grab it to hold it in the ground. Just as I did, Lou shows up just across from me. Wouldn't you know that's when it popped out! I must have hit Lou with about five gallons. Now, that wasn't the worst part. Lou was known for not getting dirty (that was my job), so when we went to lunch that day, all his oil burner buddies were getting on his case.

I think almost every Italian family has an Aunt Mary. She was always the life of the party and the first to start singing a chorus of "C'e La Luna" or "Mama" when eating stopped and the fun began. She always had something fun to say; everyone was "frigoli" and the girl cousins were "trampolines" when they dressed (how teens dressed in the 1960's). Not to mention the fact that she was a great cook, as most of my aunts were. And of course, we had the "who made the best meatballs" discussion.

For most of the 1950's and early 1960's, Aunt Mary worked at the best bakery in Corona, Queens. She worked behind the counter and her brother, my Uncle Frank, did the baking. One day, as Aunt Mary tells the story, Joe Profaci walked in with his two sons headed for the back. Apparently, Joe was wearing a white fedora at the time. Never one to miss the moment, Aunt Mary said, "There goes Charlie Chan and his two sons."

On his way out, with the boys cracking up, Profaci answered in Sicilian, "You're a real wise one."

Andy, Aunt Mary's boss, came running out and said, "Mary, don't you know who that was who you called Charlie Chan?"

She said, "yeah, Profaci, the olive oil man." Well, he was that too.

Now, an interesting side note to this story is that around the same time, my dad was a photographer for the NY Daily News in Brooklyn. For many years one of his top subjects was "Crazy Joe" Gallo, who was a member of the Profaci family. Dad would take Joe's picture often, usually on the steps of the county courthouse.

One day, probably in the mid 1960's, Joe was coming down the steps and dad was trying to take his photo. Now Joe loved being in the paper and never had an issue with having his photo taken. This time, there was a guy who kept trying to push my dad's camera away and not let him take the picture.

Finally, my dad got to ask Joe, "What's going on?"

Joe replied, "Don't worry Nick, we're going to take care of it." The following week, the guy was found in the trunk of a car on Long Island. Dad never knew the reason!

All my mom's brothers were great guys. Uncle John (Giovanni, or in Barese it was pronounced *joo-juan*) was the oldest and had a very heavy Italian accent, as he only came from Italy in the 1950's. His wife, Josephine, would make homemade traditional pasta Puglia Orecchiette that was just wonderful. I've already talked at length about Uncle Frank and Aunt Dolly. Uncle Mike was probably the funniest brother. He was big like Jackie Gleason and loved to kid around. He was always the most fun at the talent shows and gave the biggest tips to the kids. His wife, Aunt Agnes, owned a beauty parlor in Corona, Queens. My mom worked there for many years doing manicures and a few of my cousins were beauticians. I would get my haircuts there up until I was about 15. Uncle Tom was one of my favorites. He moved to College Point when I was about ten or so and I loved to go to his house on Sundays. He had three daughters and I think he liked me coming over. Uncle Tom used to let me sit on his lap and drive to my grandmother's! His wife, Aunt Ann, was a wonderful person too, and was always happy to see me. I was also close to Uncle Dom and Aunt Dot once they moved to College Point. Mainly because their son, John, was only six months older and we would hang out together. Uncle Dom used to tell my mom, "Give him a beer" when I was sixteen or so. Uncle Vic and Aunt Marge were also great, although I mostly just saw them during holidays. Aunt Marge was the only non-Italian of all the aunts and uncles.

Mom's sisters were very different. Aunt Ann was a little more strait-laced out of all the sisters and brothers. That being said, her husband, Uncle Nick, was a riot. There is one story about him that when Uncle Mike first brought Aunt Agnes home to meet the family, he asked Uncle Nick to be cool. During the course of dinner, when someone asked him to pass the chicken, he tossed it across the table.

One of the more enjoyable events that would take place was the "family meeting." Once a month, all the brothers and sisters would get together and have a big party. They did it mainly to collect money for any medical bills my grandmother might have, and just shoot the shit. For us kids it was great. I don't know how the practice started, but we got to be the bartenders, and my uncles would give us tips. Nine bucks for a 10-year-old in 1961 was big bucks, I'll have you know. It was even more fun after I turned 18 in 1969, in that when I came home from my date, I got to have a few beers with them.

Giovanni Nicoletti's Story

Giovanni Nicoletti

In late 2018, I learned that my uncle Giovanni's youngest son, Joe, had taped several conversations he had with his dad. Joe and his sister, Vita, were able to translate from the original Barese into English. Here is the summary written by Joe:

The following is a personal history of my father Giovanni (John) Nicoletti (1909-1986). I made tapes with my father in 1981 when my father was 72 years old, and this history encompasses the first 40 years of his life. We spoke in our regional Italian dialect and this translation was done by my sister, Vita, and me in December 2019. This is by necessity a summary, and many events, stories and anecdotes had to be eliminated. On occasion, I've added some explanatory notes in brackets:

I was born on May 29, 1909, in the house of my mother's parents (Francesco and Maria) in Toritto, (province of Apulia) Italy.

I was the first child of Luigi and Maria Nicoletti. My father was not there for my birth, as he was serving in the Italian army during the second Libyan war. My father was a bersalgiere (front line troops who took heavy casualties during the war), and he was one of only three that returned to Toritto in 1911. Upon his return, my father worked as watchman over flocks of sheep. In 1914 on the eve of World War I, my father was about to be recalled into the army and decided that he would go to America. My mother told him, "You were in the Army when we married, you went to war for three years missing the birth of your son, and I'm not going to be left behind."

At that time a second child had been born, Antonia (Ann), and my mother was pregnant with her third, Francesco (Frank). Feeling badly for her parents who would have no family left in Toritto (Maria's brothers Domenico and Tomasso had already emigrated and were living in New York), my parents decided to leave me behind to stay with my grandparents. They left with their daughter Ann and thought they would return in four or five years when they expected the war to be over. Once in America, their family began growing and it became difficult for them to return. They would write and send money, always wanting me to join them in America, but I was five years old when they left, and I hardly knew them. I didn't want to leave the only family I knew, my grandparents.

I went to school for about three years, but I wasn't very interested. Since school was not obligatory, I told my grandparents I didn't want to go anymore. They said, "Good, now you can go to work."

So, I began my working life at the age of seven. I did small jobs for people in town, and they would pay me with small amounts of food. Also, my grandfather had a cow, and we would go through the town selling milk directly from the cow's udder. Around that time, I also began doing small jobs at the local olive oil mill. In those days, the stone mill wheels were turned by mules, and I would groom them and hitch and unhitch them. For this work I was paid a small amount of money. Work was seasonal in Toritto, and olive season was usually December, January, and February. Olives were picked and pressed for oil, and then the trees were pruned. The other season was almonds. Usually in September they were picked, shelled, and dried in the sun. In between olive and almond season my grandfather and I would do day labor for people in town who had land. We would work in the fields, plowing, sewing, weeding, and reaping. I also maintained horses and mules and cleaned and drove carriages for the people who were better off in our town. Eventually my grandfather became too old to do field work, and I became the only breadwinner. As I grew older, I continued working at the olive mill during the season. Eventually the owner trusted me enough to make me the foreman of the place. Even though I was basically illiterate I could keep simple accounts and handle payments. During olive season, workers ate and slept at the mill, as the work started at 4 a.m. and ended at 11 p.m. This was my life in Toritto and even though we weren't rich, we were better off than many in town.

At about the age of 18, I became interested in a 15-year-old local girl named Giuseppina (Josephine) Lisi. She was well known in Toritto for her lovely singing voice. In those days, men and women connected with each other indirectly. They would use hand gestures, intermediaries, and perhaps exchange a few words at someone's house. Josephine let me know that she was interested in me, but her parents were against it. They felt that I was of a lower class than they were and wanted her to get engaged to her second cousin, who had more assets than me and my grandparents (people married class to class and finances were more important than love). Finally, I got frustrated with the whole thing and called the relationship off.

It was at that time that I began to think that I should go to America to see my parents and meet my brothers and sisters. My parents were very happy about me going over and began to organize things on their end. I got my papers together and went to the town hall to get a passport. I was shocked when they told me that I couldn't go anywhere, as I had reached draft age and was obligated to serve 18 months in the Italian army (this was in 1928). Before I left for my service I had reconciled with Josephine and her family. Even though we were now engaged, we could not be alone with each other. I would go to her house for dinner, but I couldn't sit next to her. If we went someplace in town, we always had a chaperone, usually Josephine's mother.

I was 20 years old when I went into the army, and I was stationed in Sulmona (in the Abruzzi region of Italy). During my service I reached the rank of Corporal Major. I first saw Rome when *we were assigned to guard the procession celebrating the marriage of Umberto, son of King Vittorio Emanuele. We also were*

Giuseppina Lisi and
Giovanni Nicoletti

sent to Florence to march when Benito Mussolini visited there. It was 1930 when I returned from my service and in 1931, I married Josephine. We lived with my grandparents and inherited the house when my grandparents died. It was in this house that Josephine gave birth to all her 10 children, 3 of whom died at a very young age. The Great Depression had started, and times were very difficult. I continued working at the olive mill and doing day labor the rest of the time. We had our first child, Maria (Mary), in 1931. I was 22 and Josephine was 19. By the time I reached the age of 30 we already had 5 children.

In 1938, World War II was about to break out, but fortunately for me, I was exempt from being called up because of the number of children I had. Luckily, the war basically passed Toritto by, but things were very difficult. I continued to work at anything I could find to support my family. During the war, correspondence with my parents was not possible (Italy was part of Axis) and I didn't know that 3 of my brothers were serving in the Pacific. At the end

[43]

of the war, Italy was in ruins and life was more difficult than ever, especially since my family continued to grow. A few years after the end, my mother wanted to come to Italy to see me. Her children

Uncle Giovanni and family

said that they wanted to know me also and convinced her that it would be best if I went to America to visit them. They started talking to lawyers and immigration brokers, but they all wanted money upfront with no guarantee that they could succeed. By a strange coincidence, my sister Mary overheard a conversation in a butcher shop in Corona, Queens (NYC), and introduced herself to a man named Manerino, who told her that he could get me to America. Manerino visited with my parents and said he could get me to America for $500.00 payable on my arrival. It's likely that that Manerino was an immigration broker who had political contacts. The idea was to get John over on a visa and then stay as an immigrant, allowing him to call his wife and children over. I was overjoyed when my American family informed me of their plan. They told me that Manerino would be coming to Naples on personal business, and I went there to meet with him to discuss how to proceed. He eventually came to visit me in Toritto and met Josephine and the children. After that, things became complicated and confusing, and it became clear that I couldn't go to America directly (all this took several years). Manerino finally said that the only way was for me to go to Canada. At the time it was almost impossible for Italians to get to America. Canada was much easier to enter because it needed agricultural workers. I would be contracted to work on a mushroom farm outside of Toronto for a year, after which I would be free. After some time passed and more complications arose, I was able to arrange passage on a freighter leaving from Naples and bound for Montreal. The freighter picked up cargo in Palermo and Messina, Sicily, and then Tarragona and Seville, Spain before crossing the Atlantic. 28 days later we arrived in Quebec, where immigration authorities came aboard to check our documents. There were eight passengers aboard, and when the authorities asked us if we had money (through a translator), I said I didn't, thinking that if I told them I had money they would think I was trying to get to America. The Canadian authorities, who spoke no Italian, motioned me and another passenger, who was also Italian, to get our stuff and follow them off the boat. We were placed in a building (probably an immigration facility), given cots to sleep on, and fed. Since we didn't speak English, we were confused and scared, thinking we were either in a prison or maybe an insane asylum. After two days we were brought to an office and given some Canadian money, our documents were returned, and we were escorted to a train bound for Toronto.

When I got off the train in Toronto, no one was there to meet me. All I had was the address of the man who was my contact to the mushroom farmer. With the help of a couple I met on the train who spoke Italian, I got a taxi to the address I had been given. When I arrived, the man was packed and just about to leave for Niagara Falls. He was angry, saying that he wanted nothing to do workers from Toritto, as those who had come before had caused a great deal of trouble for him and the farm owner. He eventually took pity on me and gave me the address of a boarding house (on Clinton Street) where some of my townspeople were boarding. When I got there, I called my mother; she had no idea where I was or what had happened to me. Two days later, my mother, sister Ann, and brother Frank arrived in Toronto. I was waiting at the station and recognized my mother as she got off the train. I was 40 years old, and I hadn't seen my mother in 35 years.

Giovanni meets his brothers and sisters

Mary Nicoletti's Story

Prior to getting the excerpt above from my cousin Joe, I interviewed his older sister Mary. Her account overlaps her father's recollection with great detail on life in Toritto during WWII.

What was amazing to hear was that my cousin actually knew and remembered our great-grandparents. They were probably in their mid-70's so that's something! She said that he had a bum leg, and she remembered walking behind him as he limped through town. She said that he was a good man and would bring a piece of candy when he came home.

The house she and her brothers and sisters grew up in is still there. It was originally the home of our great- grandparents and was left to my uncle, who was only four when my grandparents came to the US. She said that it was small, only two rooms. One bedroom and a large room with an open fireplace for cooking, and a curtain to make a bedroom for the kids. She said that times were tough, but they were better off than most because of the house and because my uncle owned some land.

Normally you went to school for about five years, and if you wanted to go on, you had to go to a larger town, but that was difficult as you needed to have money to take the train, which most families could not afford. During the war, school pretty much stopped. Uncle John spent some time in the army but did not serve during the war, as he had several children. She remembers the Germans coming into town very quietly and that her town was never bombed, but they would see the planes overhead and hear the bombing. They would gather up the younger kids and go into the fields, or if in Bari, go to an underground shelter. At night they would keep clothes next to the bed in case of an air raid.

She said food was very scarce; no meat, and flour was brown if you could get it, and they lived mostly on beans. After the war, Uncle John would plant, and they had a goat and would make cheese. The people would give the Americans and the Brits wine, and she said they were not nice at all, as they would get drunk and throw things and chase the girls. They would bring the Americans eggs and they would give the Italians Spam or other canned goods. She also said that there was a black market, and she would go with a neighbor to get food, but it was very dangerous, and you would be in deep trouble if caught.

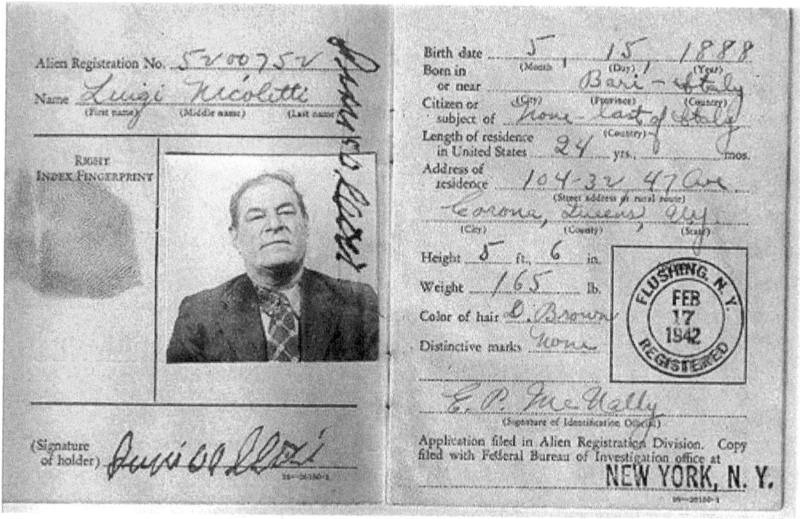
Alien Registration No. 5200752

Name Luigi Nicoletti
(First name) (Middle name) (Last name)

Right Index Fingerprint

(Signature of holder) Luigi Nicoletti

Birth date 5 (Month) 15 (Day) 1888 (Year)
Born in or near Bari - Italy
(City) (Province) (Country)
Citizen or subject of None - last of Italy
(Country)
Length of residence in United States 24 yrs. mos.
Address of residence 104-32 47 Ave
(Street address or rural route)
Corona, Queens, N.Y.
(City) (County) (State)
Height 5 ft. 6 in.
Weight 165 lb.
Color of hair D. Brown
Distinctive marks None

FLUSHING, N.Y. FEB 17 1942 REGISTERED

E. P. McNally
(Signature of Identification Officer)

Application filed in Alien Registration Division. Copy filed with Federal Bureau of Investigation office at NEW YORK, N.Y.

Luigi Nicoletti enemy alien

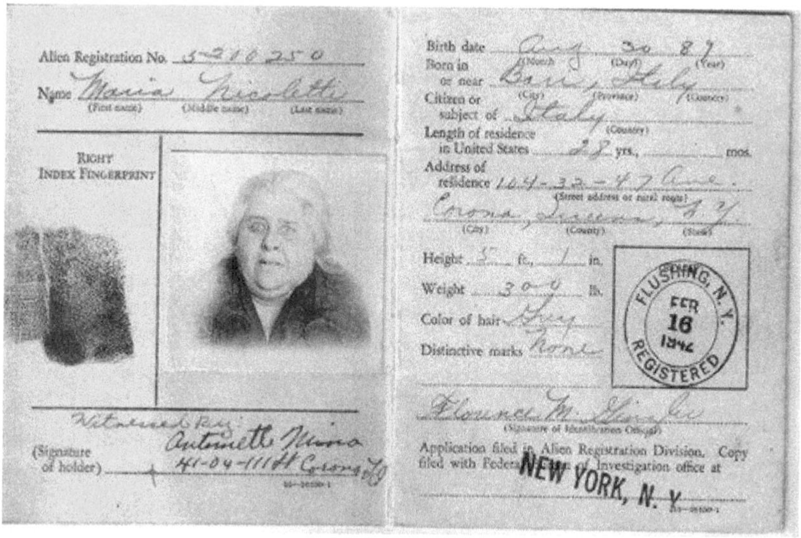
Alien Registration No. 5216250

Name Maria Nicoletti
(First name) (Middle name) (Last name)

Right Index Fingerprint

Witnessed by: Antoinette Nina 41-04-111 St Corona, L.I.
(Signature of holder) +

Birth date Aug (Month) 30 (Day) 87 (Year)
Born in or near Bari, Italy
(City) (Province) (Country)
Citizen or subject of Italy
(Country)
Length of residence in United States 28 yrs. mos.
Address of residence 104-32-47 Ave.
(Street address or rural route)
Corona, Queens, N.Y.
(City) (County) (State)
Height 5 ft. 1 in.
Weight 300 lb.
Color of hair Grey
Distinctive marks None

FLUSHING, N.Y. FEB 16 1942 REGISTERED

(Signature of Identification Officer)

Application filed in Alien Registration Division. Copy filed with Federal Bureau of Investigation office at NEW YORK, N.Y.

Maria Nicoletti enemy alien

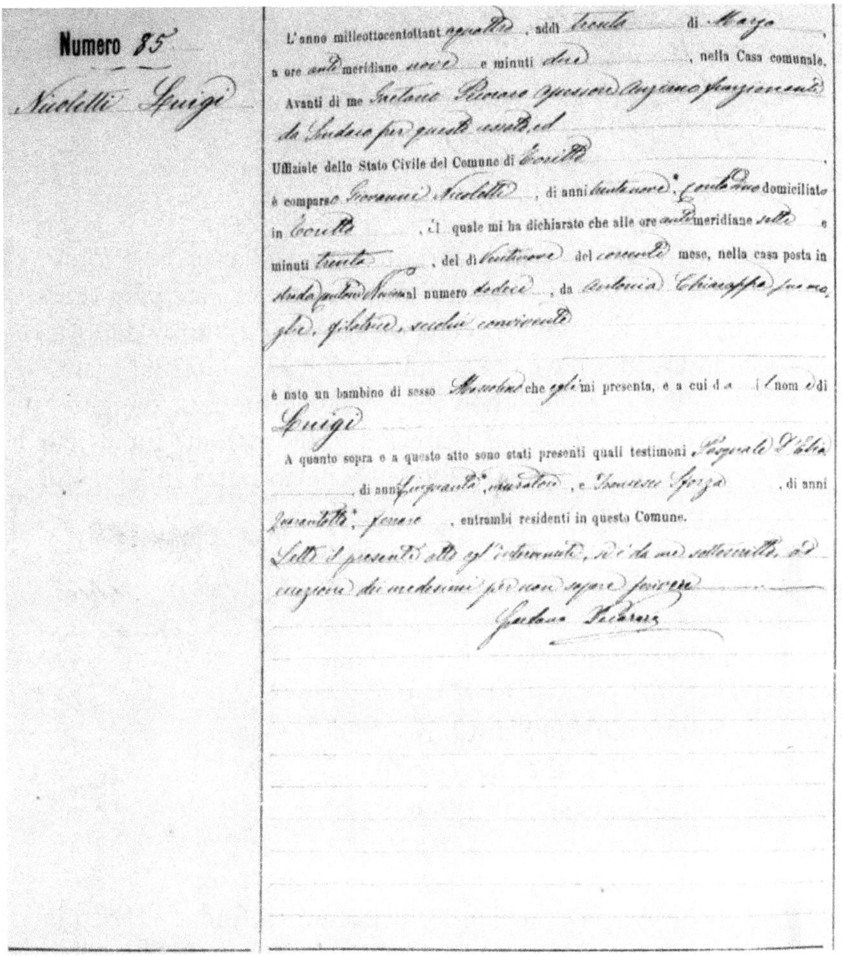

Numero *35*

Nicoletti Luigi

L'anno milleottocentottant*aquattro*, addì *trenta* di *Maggio*, a ore *anti*meridiane *nove* e minuti *due*, nella Casa comunale.

Avanti di me *Gaetano Picano* *qui... Anziano fungiormente* *da Sindaco per questo evento, ed* Uffiziale dello Stato Civile del Comune di *Bovillo*, è comparso *Giovanni Nicoletti*, di anni *ventinove*, *contadino* domiciliato in *Bovillo*, il quale mi ha dichiarato che alle ore *anti*meridiane *sette* e minuti *trenta*, del dì *venticinque* del *corrente* mese, nella casa posta in *strada ... al* numero *dodici*, da *Antonia Chiarappa* *sua moglie* *... filatrice, seclu convivente*

è nato un bambino di sesso *maschile* che *egli* mi presenta, e a cui d*à* i *nomi di*

Luigi

A quanto sopra e a questo atto sono stati presenti quali testimoni *Pasquale d'Elia*, di anni *quaranta*, *...*, e *Francesco Forza*, di anni *quarantotto*, *... ...*, entrambi residenti in questo Comune.

Letto il presente atto ...

Gaetano Picano

Birth of Luigi Nicoletti 20th of March 1884 to Giovanni Nicoletti age 29 a farmer and Antonia Chiarappa a seamstress

[49]

Piromallo

When I first searched for Nicola Piromallo on the internet, I found a record from Angelfire that showed a Nicola Piromallo marrying Emilia Caracciolo in 1882. The names seemed correct, in that my dad was the second son and would have been named after his maternal grandfather, and my aunt and godmother, Emily, being the first daughter, would have been named after her maternal grandmother. But I had never heard the name Caracciolo. I called my cousin Luisa (the second daughter of Emily and named after my grandmother), who lived with my grandparents, and asked if she knew the name. She said, "of course, that was nanny's mother." She went on to tell me that my grandmother would relate stories about her ancestry and that there was a famous admiral (Francesco Caracciolo) and Saint (also Francesco). She would also claim that her cousin was a princess. According to Luisa, they thought this was pretty much a fabrication. But it was true!

Nicola Piromallo

When I began my research, I fully expected to find that Nicola Piromallo was maybe a minor noble. The fact is, that while from a noble family, his father Saverio Giovanni did not inherit any title. It was his older brother who eventually became the Duke of Capracotta in Molise. But still being from a noble line, he did have some status. What really had me perplexed at the start was that I found a line for the Dukes of Capracotta, but the full name was Piromallo Capece Piscicelli. It appeared that I had the right family, but under Count Giacomo Piromallo and Duchess Beatrice Capece Piscicelli, I did not see Saverio Giovanni, nor his cousin Francesco or any other siblings. But I was pretty sure that I had the right family.

After years of research and eventually finding the Piromallo cousins in Italy, I realized that I did indeed have the correct family. What complicated the matter was that two events took place. First, Duchess Beatrice inherited her title from her brother, who did not have any heirs. Second, after Duchess Beatrice passed away, her son Giuseppe, who inherited the title, merged the family names. Therefore, only direct descendants are Piromallo Capece Piscicelli. I figured this out after connecting with some of my third and fourth Piromallo cousins who still reside in Italy. I found several cousins who descended from my third great-grandparents.

Index record for my great-grandfather

As I was making these connections, we were finding that we had more and more common ancestors and that they had photos of people and artifacts to share. It was amazing to see the resemblance and to find that there were still several homes standing. My third great-grandparents owned a home in Calabria, a villa in Ischia, and the current town hall of Capracotta. The villa in Ischia is still partially owned by a Piromallo.

As surprised as I was to find that I had Italian Cousins, I think the Piromallo cousins in Italy were equally as surprised to find out that they had an American cousin. I was able to put together an expanded family tree with their help and they appreciate the work and the research that I have done.

From my research and the Nobili di Napolitani (Nobility of Naples), I found that the Piromallo family came from Spain in the mid 1500's. This would have been at the beginning of the Spanish takeover of southern Italy, specifically the Kingdom of the Two Sicily's. As the Spanish noblemen arrived in Italy, they began to marry into noble Italian families. Unfortunately, I have a large gap in this family between 1500 and the early 1700's, so I am unable to connect the dots all the way back to

Domenico Piromallo, who died defending the castle of Crotone in 1528, and was the original Piromallo from Spain. (During my trip to Italy in June 2022, my cousin Cinzia gave me evidence that closed the gap.)

I have been able to trace Duchess Beatrice Capece Piscicelli back to 1781 through the Libro d'Oro. I think part of the problem in finding an unbroken link through Piromallo, is because of the merging of the two-family names in the 1800's. In fact, Capece and Piscicelli are two families that merged. This branch of the family dates to the mid 1300's.

My great-grandfather with his daughters

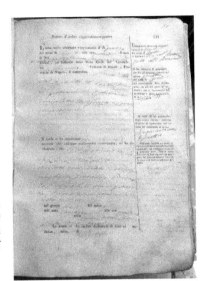

Nicola Piromallo's birth record. It shows that that he was "figlio naturale" or the illigitimate son of Saverio Giovanni Pirmallo. It also shows both of his marriages

Caracciolo

One of the great sources of documentation for anyone doing research on their Italian ancestors is the Trecanni.it. It is an Italian encyclopedia, with facts not found anywhere else. Much of what I found about my noble Italian ancestors comes from research on this site.

The Caracciolo family is one of oldest and most noble families in Naples. When I started my research, I never heard of this family, let alone know that my great-grandmother would trace me back 1,100 years, with over 100 direct ancestors.

The Caracciolo family has many branches over the centuries; it is difficult to be sure of all the genealogical connections between the different branches, however the Libro d' Oro Mediterranean does have a comprehensive list of family trees. According to tradition, the Caracciolo is Byzantine in origin and divided into three main branches: Caracciolo Rosso, Caracciolo del Sole, and Caracciolo Pisquizi. You can see below the list of all the branches:

- o Caracciolo Rosso, Caracciolo Bianchi, Caracciolo Viola: Barons and Marquesses of Pannarano
- o Caracciolo Rosso
- o Patrician Line
- o Principles of Forino
- o Counts of Pradovera and Macerato (Caracciolo of Piacenza)
- o Dukes of Vietri
- o Marquesses of Brienza
- o Princes of Avellino
- o Princes of Torchiarolo
- o Princes of Torella
- o Principles of Athena
- o Dukes of San Vito and Marquesses of Grumo
- o Dukes of Airola

[54]

- Caracciolo Pisquizi
- Princes of Torrenova and Marquesses of Casalbore
- Marquesses of Sant'Eramo
- Carlo's Line
- Lords of Pisciotta (Caracciolo d'Aragona)
- Bartholomew's line
- Principles of Santobuono
- Princes of Villa Santa Maria and Dukes of Gesso
- Dukes of Celenza
- Marsicovetere Line
- Principles of Princes of Marano
- Dukes of Castelluccio, Resigliano and Pomigliano
- Dukes of Sicignano
- Dukes of Martina, Princes of Cursi and Marquesses of Macchiagodena
- Dukes of Avigliano
- Principles of Pettoranello
- Marquesses of Gioiosa, Dukes of Girifalco, of Orta, of Soreto, of Rodi and Roccaromana and Arena
- Lords of Montanara
- Princes of Castagneto
- Dukes of Feroleto
- Caracciolo del Sole
- Barons of Accadia and Ancient Lines
- Dukes of San Teodoro and Marquesses of Villamaina
- Dukes of Miranda
- Dukes of Melfi and Counts of Sant'Angelo
- Principles of Melissano
- Dukes of Venosa[i]

Through the Libro d' Oro I have been able to trace my lineage back to Teodoro Caracciolo (919-976), the first Caracciolo listed. The founder of the Rosso line was my 26th great-grandfather Riccardo, who was known as "Rosso" who died around 1140.

The next key person is Giovanni (d. 1328). His son Filippo was the head of the Di Brienza and Vico lines. Filippo my 17th great-grandfather was a Neapolitan Patrician who was exiled from 1350-1359, but he did hold the Castle of Campello in 1363.

Filippo's son Niccolo II had some interesting titles in that he was the Castellano di Mondragone in 1367, the Captain General over all evil-doers of the Kingdom of Naples in 1373, and the Rational Master of the Kingdom in 1381.

Niccolo's son, my 15th great-grandfather, was Ciarletta. He was the Lord of Monteleone, the Castellano of Castellammare di Stabia, and the Captain of Letters of Gragnano and Pimonte. A castellano was the governor of the castle and the lord's right-hand man. He was also the Maestro Portulano of Puglia. He passed away in 1450.

His son Domizio was the Lord of Ruoti and Governor of Calabria. Domizio's son Giovanni Battista, also known as "Ingrillo," was the first Earl of Gallarte.

The last person in the ancient line is Domizio (1508-1576), who was the First Duke of Atripalda and founded the Avellino line of the family.[ii]

I descend from the Fourth Prince of Torchiarolo, Luigi. He was born in Naples on Jan 31, 1782 and died there on Feb 15, 1853. In addition to being the prince, he was the Marquis of Salcito, Marquis of Villanueva de los Torres, and the Marquis of Montenegro. In 1818 he was made Grande of Spain in the first class. He married Marquesa Costanza Saluzzo, the daughter of Prince Agostino of Santo Mauro, on May 31, 1801. His ninth son Filippo (1820 - 1868) married Elisa Mohr in 1856. Their third child was my great-grandmother Emilia, born in 1859.[iii]

The Elisa Mohr story is very interesting. She was born in Lucerne, Switzerland. I never thought that I would discover anything about her life. But I did! Doing some random searches one day, I came across a book from the mid-19th century that listed the officers in the Neapolitan Army. I found that there was a captain in the Swiss Guard with the name Martino Mohr. Going back to the Antenati, I eventually found the record of the marriage of Filippo Caracciolo to Elisa Mohr. Her name was incorrectly indexed as "Moler." Lo and behold, her father was Martino. Now, the story does not stop there. I found a site that said if you have any questions about Swiss ancestry, send us an email in German, English or Italian. I inquired about the Mohr name, and they sent me a link to the handwritten charts of all the prominent Lucerne families. There I found Elisa and Martino, enabling me to trace my Swiss ancestry back to the 1300's.

Caracciolo/Mohr

These are the records of my father's maternal grandmother, Emilia
Caracciolo di Torchiarolo:

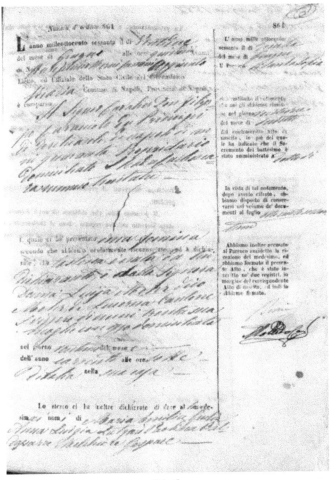

Birth

*Translation: On June 22nd, 1860, before the civil status officer of Naples, Vicaria dis-
trict, appeared Lord Knight Filippo Caracciolo of the Princes of Torchiarolo. Wealthy
aged 40, residing at 33 Carbonara Street who presented a female child whom he declared was born to him and to lady Luisa Mohr from Lucerne, Switzerland, aged 30,
his wife living with him, on the 21st of said month at 7 hours. The same also declared
to bestow to the child the names of Maria, Emilia, Giulia, Anna, Luigia, Lutgard, Pao-*

lina, Baldassarre, Melchiorre, Gaspare. Witnesses to this act were Lord Knight Ferdinando Messanelli, wealthy aged 32 from Naples, and Lord Count Francesco Cigala, wealthy aged 34 from Naples. She was baptized on June 22nd, 1860.

Side note on second page: On June 24th, 1882, Maria Emilia Caracciolo of the late Filippo married with Nicola Piromallo in the Vicaria District of Naples.

L'anno millenovecento~~due~~ , addì ~~venti~~ di ~~luglio~~

a ore ~~otto~~ meridiane ~~dieci~~ e minuti _____ , nella Casa comunale.

Avanti di me ~~Nicola Marino Vice Segretario comunale~~

~~delegazione del Sindaco del due dicembre ultimo~~

Uffiziale dello Stato Civile del Comune di ~~Napoli Vicaria~~ sono comparsi

~~Giuseppe Canetti fu Vincenzo~~ di anni ~~quaranta proprietario~~ domiciliato

~~in Via Trinchera f. Eugenio Tornatore di Antonio~~ , di anni ~~ventuno~~

~~Avvocato~~ , domiciliato in ~~Vasella Ill.e~~ i quali mi hanno dichiarato che a ore

~~3~~ meridiane ~~tre~~ e minuti _____ di ~~ieri~~ , nella casa posta in

~~Via Carbonara~~ al numero ~~trenta~~ , è morta ~~Maria Emilia Caracciolo~~

di ~~anni quarantadue gentildonna~~ , residente in ~~Napoli~~

nat~~a~~ in ~~Napoli~~ , da ~~fu Filippo~~ , domiciliato in

_____ , e da ~~fu Luisa Mohor~~ _____ , domiciliata in _____ ~~moglie di Nicola Piromallo~~ .

A quest'atto sono stati presenti quali testimoni ~~Gustavo Canestrelli di Giovanni~~

di anni ~~venti tre negoziante Giovanni Piromallo fu Francesco~~ di anni

~~cinquanta tre proprietario~~ ambi residenti in questo Comune. Letto il presente atto

a tutti gl'intervenuti ~~li medesimi lo sottoscrissero di di Corelia~~

~~colo postilla di quante te approvata~~

~~Giuseppe Canetti — Eugenia Cornatore~~

~~Gustavo Canestrelli Piromallo Giovanni~~

~~Nicola Marino~~

~~Caracciolo di Torchiarolo~~

~~Maria Emilia~~

Vice Secretary, functioning for the Mayor. Official of the ci

---

Maria Emilia Caracciolo di Torchiarolo- The year 1902, the 20th day of July, at the hour of 10 AM at the town hall. Before me Nicola Marino, Vice Secretary, functioning for the Mayor, Official of the civil state of the comune of Naples Vicaria, appeared Giuseppe Canetti (son of deceased Vincenzo), age 40, a landowner living at Via Trinchera and Eugenio Tornatore (son of Antonio), age 21. They said at the hour of 3 PM yesterday at a house at Via Carbonara number 30, the death occurred of Maria Emilia, age 42, a kind woman, who was born and lived in Naples, daughter of the deceased Filippo and the deceased Luisa Mohr, and she was the wife of Nicola Piromallo. This act was made in the presence of Gustavo Canestrelli (son of Giovanni), age 23, a merchant, and Giovanni Piromallo (son of deceased Francesco), age 53, a landowner. After reading this act to all present, they all signed with me in the margin.

[59]

As I stated earlier, the Princes of Torchiarolo are part of the Caracciolo Rosso line. The head of the Princes of Torchiarolo, Ambrogio descends from Domizio Caracciolo (1508-1576). Domizio was the First Duke of Atripalda, the First Count of Torella, and Most of the descendants of Domizio were dukes and counts through the Campania and Molise areas. They all married women from noble Italian and Spanish families. My direct line goes back through the people below:

Don Marino (D 1591) was the Second Duke of Atripalda, Second Count of Torella, and First Prince of Avellino. He married Crisotoma Carafa, the daughter of Count Fabrizio of Ruvo.

His son Don Camillo (1563-1617) was the Second Prince of Avellino, Third Duke of Atripalda, and Third Count of Torella. In 1609 he was named the Grand Chancellor of the Kingdom of Naples, and in 1602 he was named a Knight of the Golden Fleece. He was also a Counselor of War, Counselor to the Kingdom of Naples, General in the Calvary, and Governor of Calabria. He married three times and I descend from his first wife, Roberta Carafa, the daughter of Marizio, Duke of Maddaloni.[iv]

Prince Camillo

Public domain, via Wikimedia Commons

Don Camillo's son Don Marino II (1587-1630), my ninth great-grandfather, was the Third Prince of Avellino, Fourth Duke of Atripalda, First Marquis of San Severino, and First Count of Serino. In 1617 he was named the Grand Chancellor of the Kingdom of Naples, and in 1622 he was named a Knight of the Golden Fleece. He was also General Catafratti. He married two times and I descend from his second wife, Donna Francesca d'Avalos d'Aquino d'Aragona, the daughter of Prince Inigo of Francavilla.

His son, Don Francesco Marino (1631-1674), was my eighth great-grandfather and was the Fourth Prince of Avellino, Fifth Duke of Atripalda, Second Marquis of San Severino, and Second Count of Serino. In 1663 he was named a Knight of the Golden Fleece. He was also Armored General. In 1666 he married Donna Geromina Pignatelli Tagliavia d'Aragona Cortes, the daughter of Don Ettore IV, Fourth Prince of Noia and Duke of Terranova. Francesco Marino was baptized by proxy by the Infanta of Spain, Mary, Queen of Hungary, and placed under the tutelage of his uncle Tomasso, Bishop of Cyrene. Besides being an active general, he also founded the Accademia degli Inquieti, based in his palace in Atripalda.[v]

Prince Marino

Public domain, via Wikimedia Commons

His son, Don Marino Francesco (1668-1720) was the Fifth Prince of Avellino, Sixth Duke of Atripalda, Third Marquis of San Severino, and Third Count of Serino. He was the Grand Chancellor of the Kingdom of Naples in 1674 and Grande of Spain in the First Class in 1708. He was named a Knight of the Golden Fleece in 1694. He was also the First Prince and therefore qualified to be called "Highness." In 1668, he married Donna Antonia Spinola, the daughter of Don Paolo, Duke of San Severino, who brought him a dowry of 60,000 Ducati. He was only six years old when his father died, leaving him a colossal fortune. The fiefs of the house included most of today's Campania. He was educated by the best tutors in Naples and his income was thousands of Ducati a month, making the Caracciolo d'Avellino house one of the most powerful families in the Kingdom of Naples.

Marino Francesco was very impulsive and in 1687 was almost imprisoned for killing some soldiers. Five years later he was imprisoned for killing one of his vassals. At one point, he had the respect of King Philip V of Spain, but that eventually broke down. When war broke out between Spain and Austria for the Kingdom of Naples, he sided with the Austrians. In 1707, he commanded four thousand soldiers and prevented the Spanish calvary from taking the Abruzzi route. In 1710, King Charles appointed him Ambassador to Pope Clement XI. After two years he left the post and was awarded a cash bonus over his 40,000 Ducati per year. He died in 1720 in Vienna, suspected of being poisoned. His seventh child Ambrogio was the head of the Torchiarolo line.[vi]

Prince Ambrogio

Public domain, via Wikimedia Commons

Ambrogio (1699-1746) was the First Prince of Torchiarolo with the qualification of "Durchlaut" (Your serene highness). He was a Field Marshall in the Neapolitan and Spanish army, Grand Master of the Hunt of the Court of Naples, and a Knight of the Golden Fleece. He married Francesca Afan di Ribera in 1729 in Vienna.

His son and my fifth great-grandfather was Luigi (1734-1756), the Second Prince of Torchiarolo, also with the right of "Durchlaut." He married Maria Imara Francone. Their son was Ambrogio II (1755-1818), the Third Prince of Torchiarolo, Marquis of Villanueva de los Torres, Marquis of Montenegro, and Grande of Spain in the first class. He was also Prince of Pietracupa and Ripa Francone and Marquis of Salcito from his mother. He married Maria Teresa Sanchez de Luna, the daughter of Alonso, Duke of Sant'Arpino.

The fourth prince and my fourth great-grandfather was Luigi (1782-1853), who held all the titles of his father. He was married to Costanza Saluzzo, the daughter of Agostino, Prince of Santo Mauro and Duke of Corigliano. Their ninth child was Filippo (1820-1868). Filippo's daughter Emila (1859-1902) was my great-grandmother.[vii]

My 18th great-grandfather was Giovanni, known as Sergianni (1372-1432). He fought with Hungary against the Angevins and was taken prisoner in 1411. After being set free, he became the lover of

Queen Giovanna II, who made him seneschal of the kingdom. In 1418 he had to leave the kingdom, only to return the following year. With support of the pope, he removed his Sforza rival and resumed his power over the queen. Against Sforza and Louis III of Anjou, and supported by the pope, Caracciolo invoked the help of Alfonso of Aragon (1420), but when Alfonso proved to be his opponent, Caracciolo convinced the queen to adopt Louis of Anjou. Caracciolo ruled as a despot, until he was suppressed by a conspiracy, in which the queen herself took part. [1]

As I said earlier, the Caracciolo line goes back to the eighth century in Naples, with many illustrious figures. These include Saint Frances Caracciolo and Admiral Francesco Caracciolo, who fought with the British during the American Revolution and was hanged on his own ship.

Prince Sergianni

Gaudalupi, Francesco. "Palazzo Ducale - Martina Franca (TA)." Brundarte, May 6, 2017. http://www.brundarte.it/2017/02/05/palazzo-ducale-martina-franca-ta/.

Weddings

*Julia Sorrentino and
Anthony Cusumano*

*Costanzo DeMaria
and Emily Sorrentino*

Caroline Nicoletti and
Nicholas Sorrentino

*Frank Scarangella
and Mary Nicoletti*

*Dolly De Panicis and
Frank Nicoletti*

Nicholas Mina and Antoinette Nicoletti

Uncles in WWII

By the end of the war my grandparents had four sons in the war.

Michael Nicoletti

Vito Nicoletti

Dominic Nicoletti

Thomas Nicoletti

Nicholas Sorrentino

Great-Grandparents

Francesco Nicoletti, Maria Carnevale and Giovanni Nicoletti

Achille Sorrentino and Giulia Princi with grandchildren Maria, Emilia and Achille

Family

Maria Nicoletti and sons

Giovanni Nicoletti meets his brothers and sisters

Luigi Nicoletti

Luigi Nicoletti c 1958

Maria Nicoletti

Luigi and Maria Nicoletti

Nicoletti Uncles c 1942

Nicoletti brother-in-laws

Maria Luigia Piromallo
c. 1900

Maria Luigia Piromallo c. 1905

Dad

Nick Sorrentino

Maria Luigia Piromallo
with brothers and
children. Naples c 1913

Ubaldo Sorrentino and
Luigia Piromallo

45th Wedding Anniversary with Children

Sorrentino Family c 1935

Mom

Caroline Nicoletti

Piromallo Artifacts from Italy

The Noble Side

The following pages are dedicated to the noble Italian families that I have found while doing my research. It is not my intention to boast or make any claims, rather to show that through intensive research you can find a lot of interesting facts. We know a lot about the Spanish, French and British royalty, and nobility through books, tv and movies. Most of the Italian nobility has been overlooked and as a lover of history I have found these people to be just as interesting.

Through my Caracciolo grandmother, Emilia, I have discovered that not only do I descend from many Italian noble families, but also most of the European Royal Houses, such as Capet, Valois, Castile, Leon, Plantagenet and many others.

To be fair, there are millions of people around the world that descend from these royal houses, the trick is to be able to find that link. This is very difficult for those of us from Italian descent in America, as the clues have been lost. Many Americans of English descent can find these links through a "gateway ancestor". Basically, a "gateway ancestor", can be linked to British Nobility or Royalty through a direct ancestor that came to America in the 17th or early 18th century. Many of the US Presidents have "gateway ancestors". Because of the excellent record keeping in the United States, they can be fairly easy to find.

A perfect example of this is my adopted daughter. When she turned 18 we met her birth parents and her birth father was Stan Lindler. We found out that his family was in the US for centuries, so I began my research. I found out that Stan was a descendent of Daniel Boone. Daniel was a descendent of Captain Morgan the Pirate, who was from British nobility. Eventually, I discovered that Nicole is a distant cousin of Princess Diana Spencer. While it is difficult, it is not impossible to find your noble roots, if they exist.

At the beginning of each chapter there will be my take on some of interesting facts about these families and in particular my direct ancestors. For some of these families I could have added many more people, but I decided to include only the most notable. Whenever possible I have included a likeness or portrait from a well-known artist.

As you go through these pages you will find some very interesting titles and occupations, for example the Orsini family with five generations of Grand Executioners!

D'Aquino

The D'Aquino family is an ancient family dating back to around 800 AD. The family originates from Lombardy and was among the seven great houses of the kingdom. They contributed in a major way to the history of Southern Italy. You will recognize this family from Saint Thomas Aquinas who descends from a branch of this family. He is one of several Catholic of Orthodox Saints that I have found including 23 direct ancestors

This is one of the noble families where I cross lines several times. I can trace all the way back to the likely head of the family, my 35th great-grandfather, Radoaldo, who owned the city of Aquino, Terra di Lavoro (Campania). I have many ancestors with this name over about a thousand years.

My 26th great-grandfather in this line was Tomasso I (1201 - 1251) who was the First Count of Acerra, Justice of Terra di Lavoro (executioner), the Captain General of the Kingdom of Sicily, and Ambassador to the Pope. He was also the Mayor of Cremona. During this time, he made many trips to the Orient and brought back large quantities of gunpowder. His son, Adenolfo III, was the Captain General of the Imperial Troops of Lombardy.

Tomasso II (1226-1273), my 24th great-grandfather, was the Second Count of Acerra, invested by the pope and confirmed by King Conrad. He was the Valet of the Emperor in 1243 and Captain of the Duchy of Spoleto in 1249. In 1247, he married Margarita di Hohenstaufen, the daughter of HRE and King of Sicily, Federico II. In a list of feudal lords from 1271-1272, it shows that he owned Accera, Marigliano, Ottaiano, and one quarter of Posta. He also owned the Castle of Vicalvo and the Suessola Farmhouse. In 1254, his daughter Giovanna married Pietro II Ruffo, Count of Catanzaro, and they are my 23rd great-grandparents. Tomasso II was able to ascend quickly through the court, as he was the grandson of Federico II. After a brief allegiance to the pope, he aligned himself with the powerful King Conrad. [2]

From another branch of this family, my 23rd, great-grandmother, Teodora D'Aquino married Ruggero Sanservino, the Third Count of Marsico.

Through another branch, my 14th great-grandmother, Antonella, married Inigo d'Avalos d'Aragona, First Count of Monteroduni. Antonella was the Marchesa of Pescara, Contessa of Loreto and Monteroduni in her own right, and her male ancestors held many noble titles. Her father, Bernardo Gaspare was the First Marchese of Pescara. His father, Francesco II was the Fifth Count of Loretto and Justice of Abruzzo. He was also, the Grand Siniscalco of the Kingdom of Naples, and in 1438, the Grand Counselor of the Kingdom of Naples. In addition, he was the Castellano of Atina and Piedimonte. The Fourth Count of Loreto and Count of Satriano was Giacopo I (d 1423). Finally, he was the Baron of Trentola and San Marzano, and Lord of several other fiefdoms.

The next person in this line was my 18th great-grandfather, Berardo II (d 1374). He was the Cosignor to Alberto, San Donato Campoli, and Settefrati. He married Orsolina de Yels. His father, Tomasso, was the Second Count and his first wife was Tomassa di Sus. Tomasso's father Bererado started life as a cleric. Later in life, he was Lord of Albeto, San Donato, Campoli and Settefrati. He was the First Count of Loreto and Chamberlain to King Robert I of Sicily. Finally, in 1329, he was Royal Ambassador to Hungary. His father was Cristoforo I, the First Count of Ascoli and Knight of Charles II of Anjou. His father was Tomasso II mentioned above.

My 13th-generation great-grandmother, Cristotoma, came from another branch and was married to Antonio Carafa, the first earl of Ruvo.

From the D'Aquino Di Caramanico branch, my 8th great-grandmother Prudenza married Giuseppe Capece Piscicelli. Their son later became the Duke of Capracotta.[3]

D'Avalos

The d'Avalos was a Spanish family, that went to Italy with Alfonso I of Aragon in the mid 15th century. I enter this family when my 9th great-grandfather Prince Marino Caracciolo married his second wife Princess Francesca. d'Avalos.[1]

Francesca's father was Iñicco III (1578-1632), who was the fifth Marquis of Vasto, Marquis of Pescara, Prince of Francavilla and Count of Monteodorisio. In 1605, he was made a Knight of the Golden Fleece.

My 14th great-grandfather, Iñicco I d'Avalos (d. 1484). He was the son of Rodrigo Count of Ribadeo Spain. Iñicco arrived in Italy in 1442 after the arrival of Alfonso of Aragon. In 1435, he participated in the naval battle of Ponza won by the Genoese. He was Grand Chamberlain from 1449. In 1452, he married Antonella d'Aquino marquesa of Pescara, and in the same year he received the county of Monteodorisio. His power, which increased during the reign of Ferrante, laid the foundations for the family's fortune.[2]

My 12th great-grandfather Alfonso II d'Avalos (1502-1546) was born in Ischia on May 25, 1502, from one of the most illustrious families of the Kingdom of Naples, son of Iñicco (II), Marquis del Vasto, and Laura Sanseverino. Orphaned early, he was educated by his aunt Costanza, Princess of Francavilla, and is famous for having defended the island of Ischia against the French in 1593. Linked by great affection and friendship to his eldest cousin Ferdinando Francesco, the famous marquis of Pescara. He took to the military very young, took part in the battle of the Bicocca in 1522 and distinguished himself during this campaign in the conquest of Lodi and the occupation of Genoa. Under the command of an Italian infantry unit, he took part in the unfortunate campaign of

Provence in 1524 and fought at the siege of Marseille, during the retreat he was temporarily entrusted by the Marquis of Pescara with the command of the imperial infantry, and he successfully directed the retreat from Acqui Terme to Pavia.

Titian, Public domain, via Wikimedia Commons

An important role that he had was in the battle of Pavia (February 24, 1525), in which he commanded the vanguard of the imperial army, consisting of fifteen hundred foot soldiers and as many soldiers with firearms. With these forces having made a breach in the wall of the port of Mirabello, he attacked the left wing of the opposing army and valiantly sustained the impact of the gendarmerie and the French, until the intervention of the bulk of the imperial army successfully ended the battle. After this, he was commissioned by the Marquis of Pescara to occupy the marquisate of Saluzzo, completed by July 1525.

For these enterprises, at the request of his cousin, he obtained from the emperor, the nomination as General Captain of all the infantry of the Army of Italy (25 Nov. 1525). On the death of the Marquis of Pescara, which occurred in the same year, he inherited the fiefdoms and the title of marquis and later in 1528, the titles of prince of Francavilla and Count of Montescaglioso and Belcastro were added, and the office of governor of Ischia, inherited from his aunt Costanza. Together with Antonio de Leyva, in 1526, he forced Duke Francesco II Sforza to abandon Milan and renounce any anti-imperial attempt.

In February 1529, he led the Spanish and Italian infantry from Rome to the rescue of Naples. He assumed the direction of the imperial army against the forces of the French, Florentine, and Venetian coalition, who, under the command of Renzo da Ceri, had brought the war to Puglia. During this campaign, He failed to achieve any major success and besieged Monopoli in vain for two months.

In September 1529, he led five thousand Spanish infantrymen from Puglia to Tuscany, to the war for the Medici restoration in Florence. He distinguished himself by conquering Cortona (14 September 1529), Prato (February 1530) and Empoli (29 May 1530), which he sacked. Fabrizio Maramaldo who was besieging Volterra, requested his help and he went there and took command of the siege. The defeat inflicted on the imperials by Francesco Ferrucci, put him in such a state of fury that he abandoned the war and returned to Naples. In 1532, he enlisted a body of six thousand infantrymen to be brought to the aid of Ferdinand of Habsburg in the war with the Turks, but their retreat to Belgrade dissuaded him from the project.

In 1535, Charles V organized a great expedition against Tunis, he entrusted its direction to the Iñicco. This was one of his best military enterprises, which, under the command of twenty-five thousand infantrymen and two thousand Italian, German, and Spanish Calvary he conquered Goletta on 14 July, after having subjected it to a massive bombing. On July 16, he faced and defeated the eighty-thousand men of Barbarossa at Tunis and on July 20, also due to the contemporary insurrection of Christian slaves, he conquered Tunis by carrying out a frightening massacre of the inhabitants.

After Tunis, he contacted the imperial army in Lombardy, which was about to invade Provence, and tried in vain to advise against the undertaking which, owing to the experience made in 1524, he thought would have an uncertain outcome. Charles V instead preferred to follow the advice of Antonio de Leyva and in July 1536, he began the expedition. Iñicco was placed at the head of the infantry under the general command of Antonio de Leyva. His pessimistic predictions were amply confirmed, as a retreat was ordered.

In 1537, a devastating military revolt took place, with troops attacking Valenza and Tortona. Once this issue was resolved and upon the death of Marino Caracciolo in 1538, Iñicco was made the Governor of Milan and Commander of the Army of Italy. In 1539, Charles V accused him of various financial misdeeds and sent auditors to examine his books. In 1543, he was defeated at the battle of Ceresole Alba, losing 12,000 men and having 3,000 captured. As a result, he lost the favor of the Emperor and died a bitter man in Vigevano on March 31, 1546.[3]

D'Aragona

While the Aragonas were Spanish, I felt it was important to include them as they ruled Naples for many years and married into many of the Italian Noble families. Through this connection, I descend directly from kings and queens of Spain and Portugal. This family is very famous and as you will see below, King Ferrante of Naples believed in keeping his enemies close, very close.

Ferdinand I, my 16th great-grandfather (1379-1416) was the Infanta of Castile and Leon. In 1410, during the war with Muslim Granada, he captured the fortress of Antequera, which insured his election to the throne and was supported by the antipope Benedict XIII.[1] He accepted the crown of Aragon on June 24th, 1412, and was King of Aragon, Valenza, Sicily and Sardinia.[2]

Jaume Mateu, Public domain, via Wikimedia Commons

His son, Alfonso V "The Magnanimous" (1394-1458) was my 15th great-grandfather. He was King of Aragon (1416-1458) and King of Naples as Alfonso I (1442-1458). Alfonso was raised in the Castilian Royal Court at Medina del Campo. At the age of 21, he married Maria, Henry II of Castile's daughter and his cousin, but they did not have any children.

In 1420, he sailed with a fleet to attack Corsica in order to pacify Sicily and Sardinia. In 1421, the childless queen of Naples, Giovanna II, adopted Alfonso and named him as her heir, which she later repudiated. He liberated Naples in 1421, to great fanfare. He was tempted to intervene in Naples once again in 1432 and camped for two years in Sicily preparing his army and navy. In 1435, the Genovese defeated him at the island of Ponza, where he was captured and held prisoner in Genoa and later in Milan. He was able to charm the Duke of Milan, Filippo Visconti and in an alliance with him went back to gain possession of Naples, which he did in 1442. Naples became a center of art and culture in 1443, when Alfonso moved his court there.

To protect commerce and defend Christianity Alfonso was proactive in the Balkans Africa, and the eastern Mediterranean. However, he could not prevent the fall of Constantinople in 1453. While this was happening, Spain was suffering from serious unrest. The family estates in Castile suffered, but Valencia flourished. He was an active soldier to the end when he assaulted Genoa in 1458. He was praised, respected, and admired during his time and the next generation.[3]

Alfonso was succeeded by my 14th great-grandfather Ferrante I (1423-1494), his illegitimate son by Giraldona Carlino. In 1458, the barons revolted, and they attempted to install Rene of Anjou in his place. By 1464 he put down the rebellion,

but was still under threat from Ottoman expansion, other Italian states, and his own barons. In 1480, the Turks seized Otranto, but he was able to expel them in 1481. The barons revolted once again from 1485-1487 and wanted to replace him with Renee II of Lorraine or Frederick of Aragon, who was Ferrante's second son. At the same time Pope Innocent VIII also wanted war on Ferrante, however in 1486 he called for peace. Ferrante was able to repress this revolt by arresting and trying the perpetrators, and then confiscating lands and holding executions.[4]

I descend from his first wife, Isabella di Chiaramonte, Princess of Taranto, daughter and heir of Prince Tristano and Caterina Orsini. Their daughter Eleonora married Ercole d'Este Duke of Ferrara, Modena and Reggio.[5] All in all, he had eighteen children by several wives and concubines.

Ferrante was known to be notorious for keeping enemies close, either alive in well-guarded prisons, or dead, embalmed, in costume seated around the table. Apparently, he took great pleasure in showing them off to his guests. There is a scene in" The Borgia's" that shows this in detail.[6]

Attributed to Luigi Primo, Public domain, via Wikimedia Commons

I also descend from his son, Fernando (1494-1549) and his daughter Eleonora (1450-1493).

Fernando was my 13th great-grandfather. He was the illegitimate child of Ferrante and Diana Guardato. He was the first Duke of Montalto and later bought the county of Belcastro and baronies of Cropani and Zagarise. He was married twice, and I descend from his second wife, Caterina de Cardona daughter of Raimondo Duke of Somma.[7]

Eleonora, my 14th great-grandmother became the duchess of Ferrara when she married Ercole d'Este in 1473. Together they had six children, the most famous being Isabella d'Este. Passing through Rome, as a Princess of Naples, she was received with great fanfare. The two Borgia Cardinals, hoping to make a grand impression upon her as she travelled north to marry Ercole put her up in a lavish apartment, and held a grand banquet for her. Her legacy is that of an intelligent and educated woman. She was politically astute and would rule Ferrara in Ercole's absence. [8]

Cosmè Tura (?), Public domain, via Wikimedia Commons

d'Este

The d'Este family traces back to Alberto Azzo II (996-1097), who was my 22nd great grandfather. Azzo (1205-1264) was my 21st great-grandfather and the first Lord of Ferrara. I enter this line with my 13th great-grandmother Isabella d'Este, who married Francesco Gonzaga.

Titian, CC BY-SA 3.0 <https://crea-tivecommons.org/licenses/by-sa/3.0>, via Wikimedia Commons

Of all the people that I have found in my direct line, I think this couple is among the most intriguing. I had never heard of them before my research, much less knew that they were my ancestors. What makes them so interesting were their ties to several other historical people, such as Pope Alexander IV (the Borgia pope) and his daughter Lucrezia Borgia. Francesco had a long affair with Lucrezia Borgia, beginning in 1503, who happened to be his sister-in-law. He was the Marquis of Mantua, and a "condottiero" (mercenary captain). He was also considered the finest knight in Italy.

Isabella far outdid her husband in terms of accomplishments and being a renaissance woman. As a woman of fashion and dedicated to the arts she was admired and copied throughout Italy and France. I like to refer to her as the "Jackie Kennedy" of the 1500's. The poet Ariosto labeled her as the "liberal and magnanimous Isabella", while author Matteo Bandello described her as having been "supreme among women". Diplomat Niccolò da Correggio went even further by hailing her as "The First Lady of the world". Francesco and Isabela had eight children together, two of whom are also great grandparents, Eleonora and Federico.[1]

"Isabella d'Este was the Marchioness of Mantua, Italy from 1490-1519. Recognized as the "First Lady of the Renaissance." Isabella is famous for her patronage of the arts, literature, and music, during the high Renaissance.

Born in 1474 at the Este Castle in Ferrara, she was a brilliant child that astonished instructors. At the age of six, a marriage was arranged by her royal family. Creating a military alliance with Mantua. The Marquees of Mantua held the powerful position, Captain of the Papal Army. In 1490 at the age of 15, Isabella d'Este married Francesco Gonzaga, the Marquessa of Mantua.

In 1491, Isabella's younger sister, Beatrice, married the Regent of Milan. The regent, Ludovico Sforza, was the acting ruler of Milan and patron of Leonardo da Vinci. Isabella was introduced to Leonardo through her sister at the court of Milan. Where Leonardo worked as an engineer, artist and teacher to a small group of apprentices.

While working for Ludovico, Leonardo created the Gran Cavallo (Sforza Monument), The Last Suppe and Lady with Ermine, a portrait of Ludovico's mistress, Cecilia Gallerani. Invented weapons and fortifications for the city. In addition to designing decorations for the Sforza Castle, festivals in Milan and theatrical performances.

In 1498, Isabella decided to seek the best portrait painter to capture her image. Judging portraits by Bellini and Leonardo. Isabella requesting the loan of Lady with Ermine, from Cecilia Gallerani. Cecilia sent the painting to Mantua. Where Isabella determined Leonardo to be the winner of her contest. Unable to release himself from the demands of Ludovico. Leonardo remained in Milan until French forces invaded in 1499.

After the invasion, several Milanese took refuge in Isabella's nearby castle of Mantua. The natural aquatic fortification of the city and the military position of the Marquis of Mantua led many to find shelter within the walls of the Castello di San Giorgio. Including Cecilia Gallerani, Leonardo da Vinci, Luca Pacioli and Duchess Isabella d'Aragona.

During his stay in Mantua, Leonardo began the portrait of Isabella. Finishing two masterful sketches of the 25-year-old Marchioness. Leaving one for Isabella. Leonardo took the second, as he traveled on the Venice. The musician Lorenzo Pavia wrote Isabella in March of

1500, "Leonardo Vinci is in Venice, and has shown me a portrait of Your Highness, which is exactly like you, and is so well done that it is not possible for it to be better."

In April of 1501, Leonardo contacted Isabella through Frater Petrus de Novellara. *"If he can, as he hopes, end his engagement with the King of France without displeasing him by the end of the month at the latest, he would rather serve Your Excellency than any other person in the world."* Concluding, *"He will do your portrait immediately."* Later that month, Isabella received news from Leonardo, through her father's envoy in Florence, Manfredo de Manfredi. *"All he could say for the moment was that I might send you word that he has begun what Your Highness desired."*

In 1504, Isabella writes Leonardo thanking him in a letter. *"We shall remain so deeply obliged to you that our sole desire will be to do what you wish, and from this time for the we are ready to do your service and pleaure."* Correspondence between Isabella and Leonardo begin with his departure from Milan and continue until his return in 1506.

In April of 1507, Isabella was invited to Milan for the festival of the French King Louis XII. Where a tournament was given in her honor. Leonardo was present at the King's request, to create triumphal arches and arrange court pageants. Isabella and Leonardo, once again, assembled at the court in Milan. Provided the opportunity for Isabella to see her portrait, Leonardo brought with him. After this visit, there are no further inquiries about her portrait. It is hard to image the elation Isabella must have felt. When Leonardo revealed the unimaginable beauty he created, reflecting her image.

Isabella spent the rest of her life supporting and fostering geniuses of the high Renaissance. However, none would compare to the brilliance exhibited by the Great Leonardo. Capable of immortalizing subject and artist, in the world's most celebrated painting." *isabelladeste.org no author.[2]*

Isabella's father was Ercole (1431-1505) the Duke of Ferrara. He studied at the court of Alfonso the King of Aragon and Naples. In 1473, he married Eleonora of Aragon, the daughter of Ferdinand I of Naples. Building a very powerful alliance. From 1482 to 1484 he fought a war with Venice who were aligned with Pope Sixtus IV.

Throughout his life, he was a patron of the arts. Under Ercole, Ferrara doubled in size, with many of the most famous buildings from his reign still standing. He also admired the infamous Savonarola, also from Ferrara. Ercole petioned the Florenine church to free Savonarola without success. [3]

Ercole's father was Niccolo III (1383-1441). He inherited the city in 1393 at ten years old. In 1395, a relative, Azzo d'Este attacked the city, contesting Niccolo's right to rule. In 1397, he married Gigliola da Carrara. He had his second wife executed in 1425, for having an affair with his illegitimate son Ugo. At the same time, he decreed that all women in Ferrara found guilty of adultery be put to death, but he later rescinded the order. Ercole's mother was Ricciarda of Saluzzo. All in all, he had sixteen children, eleven of which were illegitimate. [4]

Dosso Dossi, Public domain, via Wikimedia Commons

Niccolo's father was Alberto (1347-1393) Lord of Ferrara and Modena. He also founded the University of Ferrara in 1391. [5]

Obizzo III (1294-1352) was the Marquis of Este and Lord of Ferrara in 1317. In 1336 he was Lord of Modena. He married Giacoma Pepoli.[6]

Amadio da Milano, CC0, via Wikimedia Commons

Unknown author, Public domain, via Wikimedia Commons

Capece

The Capece family originated in Sorrento and settled in Naples at the time of King Manfredi. After a brief exile, during the time of Charles I Anjou, they returned to Naples with considerable power through alliances with other families and various marriages.[1] Next to the Caracciolo family, Capece and their alliances make up much of my ancestry, from Naples and the surrounding area. They held the "Seat of Capuana" in Naples.

As I mentioned in an earlier chapter, my 3rd great-grandmother was Beatrice Capece Piscicelli. Her father was Carlo (1758-1773) who was the sixth Duke of Capracotta. He married Mariangela De Riso, from the Barons of Carpinone. Carlo's father was Giacomo (1727-1777) the 5th duke who was married to Maria Anna Capece Zurlo, the daughter of Prince Giovanni Antonio and Teresa di Capua from the Dukes of San Cipriano. The fourth duke was Giuseppe (1696-1755) married to Beatrice Sanfelice, the daughter of the Lord of Acquavella. Giacomo (1650-1711) was the third duke, and he was married to Francesca Filangieri the daughter of Carlo and Cornelia Caracciolo of the lords of Montesardo. His father was Giuseppe, the first duke married to Prudenzia d'Aquino the daughter of Tomasso Duke of Casoli.

Andrea (b 1566) was my 9th great-grandfather in this line. His father was Giovanni Battista who was married to Ortensia Caracciolo the daughter of Ferdinando and Isabella Pignatelli. Ottinello, my 15th great-grandfather in this line was in the service of King Ferdinand I of Naples. Ottinello's father, Andrea was a calvary knight and accompanied Giacomo di Borbone, the count of Marche when he came to Naples. He married Beatrice Latro the daughter of the viceroy of Naples.[2]

Maria Anna Capece Zurlo (1736-1762) comes from a different, and more prestigious, branch of this family. Her father was Giovanni Antonio (1700-1768) the second prince Capece Zurlo. He was married to Teresa di Capua the daughter of Domenico the Baron of Strambone and Ippolita del Tufo of the dukes of San Cipriano. His father was Giacomo (1669-1735) the first Prince Capece Zurlo I descend from his first wife, Ippolita Sambiase, Ippolita's mother was the third Duchess of Crosia.

My 15th great-grandfather in this line was Giovanni (d 1424) also known as "Giovannello." He was the first Earl of Sant'Angelo dei Lombardi and Potenza. He was also lord of over several other fiefdoms. He was assassinated in 1424 and his brother inherited some of his lands. He was married to Adelasia, the daughter of Ugolotto Lord of Toritto, who brought a dowry of 500 ounces of silver. Giovanni's father was Salvatore (d 1404) Seneschal of the Kingdom of Sicily under Ladislao I.

Salvatore's father was Berardo (d 1415) the first Earl of Montoro, he was also the first Earl of Nocera dei Pagani and Seneschal and Royal Chamberlain of the Kingdom of Sicily all in 1405. In 1407, he was the head of the kingdom. He was also lord of several other fiefdoms. He was married to Luigia Caracciolo, daughter of Leonetto Lord of Pisciotta and Caterina

Carafa

The Carafa family began with my 23rd great-grandfather Gregorio Caracciolo who possessed fiefdoms in Naples, Acerra and Aversa. He was married to Maria Pignatelli.

Gregorio's son Bartolomeo (d 1220) was Lord of Ripalonga and married Laura Capece, their son Filippo was also Lord of Ripalonga. It is Filippo's grandson Bartolomeo (d 1362) that begins a long line of titles to the family. He was Viceroy of Basilicata in 1302 and Master of the Kingdom of Sicily in 1309. Also, in the same year, Councilor and Royal Chamberlain and Captain General of Abruzzo. In 1343, he was Master of the Grand Court. He married Mabilia Montefalcione. He had an income of 10 ounces of gold.[1]

Two of Bartolomeo's sons are 18th great-grandfathers Andrea and Tomasso.

Andrea was Lord of Forli and Viceroy of Abruzzo in 1357. Later, he was Royal Councilor, Master of the House of Pope Urban VI and Governor of Spoleto. He was married to Maria de Cornay. His son Giacomo was Lord of Roccacinquemiglia and married Francesca Cantelmo. Their son Onfrio was also Lord of Roccacinquemiglia and in 1419 was made Captain for life of Roccacinquemiglia. In 1419, he had an income of 100 ounces. He married Caterina Carafa. Their son Giacomo started the Princes of Roccella and Counts Grotteria.

Giacomo (d 1489) was Lord of Castelvetere, Roccella and Savuto. He was the first Count of Matera and bought Gioia for 3000 Ducati. He married Antionette of Molise. Their third child, Giovanni founded the Counts of Policastro and Dukes of Forli lines.

Giovanni (d 1530) was known as "la morte" (due to his ugly appearance). He was Lord of Rofrano. In 1496, he was ambassador to Venice and in 1498 ambassador to Hungary. He was the first Count to

Policastro and bought Roccagloriosa in 1501, he also owned several other fiefdoms. He married Antonella di Castelnuovo. [2]

My 13th great-grandfather was Pierantonio (d 1532) murdered over an issue with a woman. He was the second Count of Policastro as well as Lord over his father's fiefdoms. He had an income of 400 Ducati. He was married twice. His first wife Laura dei Tolomei was my 13th great-grandmother and brought a dowry of 8000 Ducati. Their daughter, Portia married Fabrizio Carafa the Earl of Ruvo.

Tomasso's grandson, Antonio (1373-1437) started the Carafe della Stadera branch. He was known as "Malizia" and was the Lord Executioner of Bari in 1400, he bought the land of Mecurio the same year. He was the lord of several fiefdoms and Royal Chamberlain in 1410. He was made Castellano of Torre del Greco in 1420 thanks to a pledge to the Queen of Naples and was also ambassador to Aragon. He had an income of 800 ounces of gold from the trade routes of the Kingdom of Sicily. He was a famous Neapolitan diplomat and a favorite of King Alfonso V. He was married to Caterina Farafalla. Two of their sons are my great-grandfathers. Francesco (1412-1496) was my 15th great-grandfather and Lord and Captain of Torre del Greco, Portici and Resina. He married Maria Origlia. Their son, Fabrizio (d 1513) started the Dukes of Andria line. Fabrizio was the Lord of Torre del Greco, Valenzano and Sant'Eramo. He was the Cupbearer to the Duke of Calabria and Governor of Mazzara in 1455. In 1463, he was Captain and Castellano of Catanzaro. He married twice, and I descend from his first wife Aurelia Tolomeis. Their son Antonio (1471-1522) was the second Earl of Ruvo and Lord of Sant'Eramo. He married Crisostomo Aquino who brought a dowry of 4000 Ducati.

My 12th great-grandfather in this line was Fabrizio (1515-1554) who was the third Count of Ruvo. He owned over a half dozen fiefdoms. He bought the fiefdom of Andria he applied for the recognition of Duke but died before his appointment. He was married to Porzia Carafa daughter of the Count of Policastro. Their daughter, Chrysostom (1542-1591) who married Prince Marino Caracciolo of Avellino in 1557, which is where I enter the family.[3]

I also enter this family through another 10th great-grandmother, Roberta Carafa, from the Dukes of Maddaloni (1565-1603) who married Prince Camillo Caracciolo. Her father was Marzio I the second duke.

Carrara

The Cararra's were the feudal lords that came from the village of Carrara. The also ruled Padua and surrounding countryside. At first, they supported the Ghibelline's and later were Guelph leaders. The progenitor of the line was Jacopo da Carrara, who was made perpetual Captain General of Padua in 1318. They ruled for about 50 years without any serious rivals, except for within the family.[viii] His daughter Taddea married Mastino II della Scala and was my 20th great-grandmother.

Jacopo II (d 1350) was my 20th great-grandfather. He was Captain of the People of Padua from 1345, although he assumed power through forged documents and the murder of Prince Papafava. He in turn was assassinated in 1350.[ix]

His son Francesco (1325-1393) called "Il Vecchio" assumed power in 1350 and ruled until 1388. In 1356, he was named Imperial Vicar by Charles IV. In 1360, Louis I of Hungary gave him the cities of Feltre and Belluno. He fought a fruitless war against Venice, and after a war with Genoa in 1381, Leopold of Austria gave him the city of Treviso. In 1385, he allied with the Visconti of Milan against Verona. In 1388, Venice and Milan formed a coalition against him, and he was forced to abdicate in favor of his son, Francesco Novello and was forced into exile. He died in jail in Monza. His daughter, Cecilia married Wenceslaus I Duke of Saxony.[x]

Caetani

The Caetani family is an ancient family from Naples from the Seat of Nido. They held numerous titles and positions in civil, military, and religious fields, including Pope Gregory II. The First Duke of Gaeta was Giovanni (877-915). The family branched out to Pisa, where they became a very important family. [1]

The earliest ancestor I have found that I can verify is my 26th great-grandfather Giovanni (d 1167).

My 22nd great-grandfather Gofreddo (1225-1296) was the first Earl of Caserta in 1288. He was also Lord of Calvi, Vairano, and Norma. As Lord of Caserta, he owned the castles of Ducenta, Atino, Presenzano, Fontana, Vairano, and Calvi. He was a Senator of Rome from 1290-1292. He married Elisabetta Orsini.

Gofreddo's son Pietro was Counselor to the King of Naples and bought many fiefdoms in the countryside. He was Mayor of Orvieto, Marquis of Marca d'Acona, and Lord of the Fortress and land of Sermoneta. He was assassinated at Ceccano in 1308.

Next in line was another Gofreddo, my 20th great-grandfather (d 1335). He was known as "il Conticello" and was the Canon of Santo Stefano di Sgurgola. He was also the Count of Fondi and Lord of Selvamolle, Torre, Trivigliano, Trevi, Filettino, Vallepietra, and Carpino. From 1300 to 1303, he was the Rector of Campagna and Marittima. In 1322, he was the Mayor of Siena, and in 1324 he was the Captain General of Sperlonga and Castellammare di Stabia. He was married three times. His second wife, my 20th great-grandmother, was Giovanna dell'Aquila. She was the daughter of Riccardo, Count of Fondi, and Giacoma Ruffo of the Counts of Catanzaro. Gofreddo's son Niccolo (1310-1348) was the second Count of Fondi and Grand Chamberlain of the Kingdom of Naples. [2]

Niccolo's son Giacomo (1338-1423) was the founder of the Caetani dell'Aquila branch. He was Lord of Spigno, San Felice, and Ninfa, along with several other fiefdoms during his lifetime. However, the rights to many of them were steeped in controversy. He married Sveva Sanseverino in 1360. [3]

Another 19th great-grandfather, Giacomo's son Cristoforo (d 1439), was the start of the Caetani Dell'Aquila D'Aragona branch. He was the Fifth Earl of Fondi and Lord of Piedimonte, from his mother with Royal consent. He was the First Earl of Morcone, again granted by his mother. He was the Viceroy of Campagna and Molise in 1406, and the Guardian of Rome on behalf of the King of Naples in 1408. From 1410 through 1413, he was Viceroy of the Abruzzi and Captain of L'Aquila. He later became the Podesta of Naples. He was assassinated on the 18th of October at the siege of Naples.

His son Onorato was born out of wedlock, but later legitimized by Pope Martin V. He was the Count of Fondi and Count of Morcone, as well as the lord of over a dozen fiefdoms. His dowry to marry my 18th great-grandmother, Francesca of Capua, the daughter of Fabrizio of Capua from the Counts of Altavilla, was 2000 ducati (about $30,000 today).

Their son Baldassarre (1443-1487) was the Count of Marcone and the First Count of Traetto. He married Antonella Caracciolo, the daughter of Sergianni Duke of Venosa and Caterina Filangieri, Contessa di Avellino. Their daughter Giovanella, my 16th great-grandmother, married Girolamo Sanseverino, the second Prince of Bisignano, with a dowry of 12,000 ducati. [4]

Colonna

Colonna is a very ancient family that had it's beginning in Rome with my 32nd great-grandfather Teofillato in the late 800's AD. He was a rich Roman landowner, perhaps of Germanic origin. He was part of the Roman social class of landowners, wealthy clergy, city administrators and other state leaders that controlled Roman life from the 7th to the 11th Century.

Around 901, Teofillato held the office of Palace Judge for Emperor Louis the Blind. In 902, he was prominent in the overthrow the Antipope Christopher. From 904, he controlled Rome as the Commander of the City Militia and Administrator of the Pope's assets. Because of these two titles, he was in fact "Lord of the City" for about 20 years. In 915, he was sent by Pope John X to negotiate and alliance with the Lombard Princes of Campania against the Arabs. This event ended with the formation of a military league. Consequently, the Christian Army was victorious against the Saracens, who were forced out of Lazio forever.

Pope John X ousted Teofillato in 924 and he died in 925. He died with a vast domain of villages and lands around Rome. He was married to Theodora aka "Senatrix", who was considered to be a vicious and corrupt woman. She procured power for her husband by becoming the lover and protector of the Bishop of Cere and later Pope Sergius III.[1]

My tie to this family begins with my 8th great-grandmother, Anna Colonna (1631 - 1689) and I have over 30 ancestors from this grand family. Anna was the daughter of Marcantonio V.

Marcantonio V (d 1659) was the eighth Prince and Duke of Paliano. Prince of Castiglione, Duke of Miraglia, Marquis of Giuliana, Baron of Santa Caterina. In 1646, he was made Knight of the Golden Fleece. He married Isabella Gioeni.

His father was Filippo (1578-1639) who was Prince and Duke of Paliano. He was appointed Grand Constable of Naples in 1611 and Duke of Tagliacozzo, Count of Ceccano and the Marquis of several other places. He married Lucrezia Tomacelli in 1597 the daughter of Giacomo Lord of Galatro.

My 11th great-grandfather in this line was Fabrizio (1557-1580) Prince of Paliano and Captain in the Spanish Army. He married Anna Borromeo daughter of Gilberto the Count of Arona.

Fabrizio's father was Marcantonio II (1535-1585) and was possibly poisoned. He was the third Duke of Paliano, Grand Constable of Naples. More than that, he was Lord of at least twelve other fiefdoms. In 1561, he was Lieutenant of the Kingdom of

Pietro Novelli, Public domain, via Wikimedia Commons

Naples and in 1569, he was the first Duke of Tagliacozzo. Succeeding this, he was Viceroy of Sicily in 1577, Knight of the Order of the Golden Fleece in 1559, Papal Admiral and Captain General of the papal armies against the Turks in 1570. In 1552, he married Felice Orsini, daughter of Girolamo Lord of Bracciano.

Next in line was Ascanio I (d 1557 in prison). He was the second Duke of Paliano and Grand Constable of Naples. He was also, Marquis of Manoppello, Earl of Tagliacozzo, and Baron of Carsoli. He commanded the Spanish troops in Abruzzo in 1528. Ascanio married Giovanna d'Aragona daughter of Ferrante Duke of Montalto. His daughter Girolama married Camillo Pignatelli.

Fabrizio (1460-1520) wasCount of Tagliacozzo Lord of Genazzano, Anticoli, Arnara, Castro, Collepardo, Falvaterra, Giuliano, Morulo, Supino, Vico, Vallecorsa, Rocca di Cave, Rocca di Papa, Piglio, Roviano, Riofreddo, Nemi, Pofi, Sgurgola, Olevano and

Unknown Person, Public domain, via Wikimedia Commons

Serrone; Marquis of Atessa, Baron of Carsoli, Val di Roveto and Covaro from 1507. Lieutenant General of the Kingdom of Naples from 1501, Governor General of the Church militias in 1510, Lieutenant General of the Spanish troops in Italy in 1511, Grand Constable of the Kingdom of Naples with Dated Privilege 1516, Commander-in-Chief of the Spanish troops in Lombardy with appointment 1516, first Duke of Paliano and Marquis of Manoppello from 1519 as a famous leader and Spanish general, he was taken as a model leader by Machiavelli in his essay on the war. In 1488, he married Agnese Montefeltro daughter of Frederico I Duke of Urbino.

Scipione Pulzone, Public domain, via Wikimedia Commons

My 15th Colonna great-grandfather was Odoardo (1421-1503) who was Count of Alba and

Fabritius Columna III Dux Palliani

Public domain, via Wikimedia Commons

Celano and the first Duke of Marsi. He was also Lord of about a dozen other fiefdoms. He was married twice, the second time to my great-grandmother Filippa Conti daughter of Grato Lord of Valmonte.

Odoardo's father was Lorenzo Onfrio (d 1423 in a fire). Lord of Cave, Genazzano, Rocca di Cave and several other fiefdoms. He was also Count of Alba and Grand Camerario in the Kingdom of Naples. He married Sveva Caetani daughter of Iacobello and brought the land of Giuliano as a dowry.[2]

My 17th great-grandfather in this line was Agapito (1338-1398) Lord of Genazzano, Capranica Palestrina, Ciciliano and San Vito. He married Caterina Conti the daughter of Giovanni, Lord of Valmontone. His father Pietro (d 1377) was Lord of Genazzano, Capranica Palestrina, Ciciliano and San Vito and Senator of Rome. He was also Lord of Pisciano, Castelnuovo de Monte, Nepi, Santa Marozza, Corese, Casale, Marano and Castelmolle. He married Letizia Conti. Pietro's father, Giordano was Lord of Genazzano, Zagarolo, Gallicano, Monteporzio, Capranica, Ciciliano, and San Vito. He married Margherita Capocci the daughter of Giacomo Lord of Sant'Angelo.

Another Agapito (d 1300) was my 20th Great-grandfather, Lord of Colonna, Zagarolo, Gallicano and Monteporzio. He was a Senator of Roman 1293 and first Count of Monteporzio in 1294. Unfortunately, the family came into conflict with Pope Boniface VIII and was excommunicated and had his assets confiscated. He married Mabilia daughter of Pandolfo Savelli Lord of Albano. His father was Giovanni (d 1293) Lord of Colonna, Zagarolo, Monteporzio and Palestrina. He was Podesta of Orvieto in 1273, Senator of Rome in 1279 and Marquis Marca d'Ancona in 1288.

Domenico De Santis, Public domain, via Wikimedia Commons

My 26th great-grandfather in this line was Pietro. In a donation document made to the monastery of Monte Cassino, he claims to be Gregory III's son, who was the Count of Tusculum. Pietro married, Countess Elena of Palestrina.

Gregory III (d 1126) was the first "Colonna" and the son of Gregory II (d 1054) not much is known about him other than he was the brother of the pope. In 1044, he led an expedition that restored Pope Benedict IX to the throne. Their father was Alberico III (d between 1033/1044) his brother, Romano (Pope John XIX) made him Senator of Rome, which he declined to avoid tensions with Emperor Henry II. On the death of Pope John, he declined succession to the papal throne in favor of his son Theophilact (Benedict IX).[3]

The first Count of Tusculum was my 30th great-grandfather Gregory I (d 1002). He was the Apostolic Rector of Sant'Andrea in 980, Senator of Rome in 981 and trusted by Pope Sylvester II. He led the revolt against Emperor Otto III and elected head of the Roman Republic in 1001.

Gregory's father was Alberico II (911-954) Prince of the Romans. He inherited vast lands from Teofilatto. He was known to be ambitious and daring, and a prince highly respected by the Roman people. He gave some semblance of civil administration to Rome after centuries of anarchy and separated religious power from secular power. He was the first and only Prince of Rome and his name appeared next to the popes on coins. His son Octavian was elected John XII.

Alberico's mother Mariozza (892-933) was apparently quite a woman. Her first husband, and Alberico's father was Alberico, Duke of Spoleto and Camerino whom she married in Rome in 909. She ruled Rome from 915 to 932 imposing her politics on Popes and her lovers. She was captured by her son and held as a prisoner in a convent until her death.

Coreggio

This is a princely family that probably started with Frogerio (d around 1029) my 33rd great-grandfather, the first Sovereign Lord Coreggio. The family acquired most of its power when my 24th great-grandfather Gherado V defeated the Ghibellines in 1247. He was Podesta of Moderna in 1236, Parma in 1238 and 1247, Podesta of Reggio in 1240 and Podesta of Genoa in 1240. He married to Adelasia Rossi.[1]

The following year, he led the Guelphs against Frederick II in Parma. The family became extinct in 1711. My ties to this family begins with my 21st great-grandmother, Beatrice (1286-1321) who married Alboino Della Scala Lord of Verona in 1306.

Beatrice's father, Gilberto III (1240-1321) was Lord of Parma in 1303, with the title of "Defender of the Municipality and Conservator of the Peace", but he was expelled from Parma in 1308. In 1304, he was proclaimed Sovereign Lord of Piacenza, but was expelled from that position too. In 1312, he was Podesta of Mercanti, but was deposed in 1313. All that being said, he was Lord of several fiefdoms including Correggio and Fosdondo and Campagnola. He was an armed knight of the Emperor in 1310, Imperial Vicar of Reggio from 1311 to 1312, Captain General of Parma and Cremona. Captain General of Guelphs and Lombardy in 1319 and Vicar of Pontremoli the same year. Needless to say, he got around.

His father was Guido II (1230-1299) who was Lord Sovereign of Correggio, Lord of Campagnola, and several other fiefdoms. In 1268, he was Podesta of Genoa and Podesta of Bologna in 1270. He was Captain of the People in Florence in 1277 and Captain of the People in Modena in 1283. Also, in 1283, he was Podesta of Mantua and Captain General of the Armies of Parma in 1285. Guido was the son of Gherado V. [2]

Del Balzo

While I do not have a lot of ancestors in from this family, it was interesting to note them as the Del Balzo/De Baux family goes very far back in history. They originated in Provence and Toulouse France and go back to the lords of Baux. In the 12th century, they were made Princes of Orange. In 1277, Charles of Anjou gave Bertrando the county of Avellino and other lands in Campania. Their greatest power was in the fourteenth century, however this branch of family died out in 1426.[1]

I enter this line with my 21st great-grandmother Sveva (1300-1336) who married Roberto Orsini Count of Nola and brought 400 ounces of gold or silver as her dowry. Sveva's father was Hugh (d 1319) who died at the siege of Alexandria. He was Lord of Gaudissart, Count of Soleto in 1301, Lord of Laurito 1303, Lord of Sternatia, Zollino and Soleto in 1304. He was Royal Chamberlain in 1302, the Castellano di Castellammare di Stabia in 1308, Grand Seneschal of the Kingdom of Sicily in 1308 and 1310/1311, Seneschal of Piedmont 1310/1319, Royal Councilor in 1311, Vicar General of Piedmont in 1311, Grand Executioner and Treasurer of the Kingdom of Sicily 1312, Seneschal of Lombardy 1312/1314, and Lieutenant General in Lombardy 1313/1314. He was married to Jacopa della Marra.

Hugh's father was Bertrando III (d 1305), was the Prince of Orange, the lord of Courtson, Suze, Soliere, and Wissant. He died in the Holy Land. His father was Raimondo II (d 1278) and his father was William I (d 1239 and his father was William I known as "du coronet" (d 1218) all Princes of Orange.[2]

What is interesting in this family is that son of Roberto Orsini and Sveva Del Balzo used the name of both families, and his descendants were Orsini Del Balzo. Nicola (1331-1399) was my 20th great-grandfather, and condottieri that followed Cardinal Albornoz. He was Senator of Rome in 1356, Gonfalonier of the Church in 1365 and Governor of the Heritage in 1371. He was also the Count of Nola.[3]

Nicola's, second son, and my 19th great-grandfather was Raimandello (d 1406). Not having any rights of inheritance, he went to war. Upon returning, he violently took possession of the family properties. He sided with Louis I Anjou and married Maria d'Enghien, the

Countess of Lecce in 1384 and enlarged his fiefdoms. In 1399, he conquered the principality of Taranto and made it a lively center of culture and the arts.[4] His daughter, Cecilia married Antonio Sanseverino.

Della Rovere

The Della Rovere family was a humble Savoy family that became important when Francesco Della Rovere was elected Pope Sixtus IV in 1471. In 1472, he arranged for his brother Bartolomeo to marry the daughter of King Ferrante d'Aragona of Naples. Another Della Rovere Giuliano, was also elected pope with the name Julius II.[1]

I enter this family through my 11th great-grandmother Lavinia (1558-1631). Her parents were Guidobaldo II and Vittoria Farnese. She grew up in the castles of the Imperiale and Gradara families and the courts of Pesaro and Urbino. She lived for ten years in the court of her brother Francesco Maria until marrying Alfonso Felice d'Avalos d'Aquino in 1583. Alfonso was a libertine and extravagant who left Lavinia in debt for 600,000 scudi when he died in 1593. She retired to the monastery of Saint Chiara in Urbino until 1606. By the will of the Duke, she then had to establish residency in the castle of Montebello and was appointed heir of the garden and the house of Montebello after his death in 1628.[2]

Workshop of Federico Barocci, Public domain, via Wikimedia Commons

Guidobaldo (1514-1574) was the Duke of Urbino from 1538, when his father was assassinated until his death, in 1574. In 1546, he was a military leader in Venice. Guidobaldo married Vittoria Farnese in 1548. Her father was Pier Luigi Farnese. He was the Papal Governor of Fano and Captain General of the Papal States. He was also Prefect of Rome. The King of Spain contracted with him to fight against the Ottoman Turks, in 1559. In 1573, he surpassed a revolt in Urbino by the citizens over his excessive tax burden levied on Urbino.[3]

Metropolitan Museum of Art, CC0, via Wikimedia Commons

Francesco Della Rovere (1490 -1538) was Guidobaldo's father. Francesco, was the nephew of Pope Julius II. He married Eleonora Gonzaga, in 1508, the daughter of Francesco II Gonzaga and Isabella d'Este, and became Duke of Urbino. In 1509, he was promoted to Captain General of the Papal States. He then waged war against Ferrara and Venice. Failing to vanquish Bologna in 1511, he had his adversary Cardinal Alidosi executed in a brutal action. In 1513 he was made Lord of Pesaro. Under the new pope, Leo X, he lost Pesaro and in 1516, he was excommunicated by the pope and exiled from Urbino, only to return in 1521 when Pope Leo died. That same year, he was Captain General of Republic of Venice, however Pope Clement VII had him marginalized. He was poisoned in 1538 and died in Pesaro.[4]

Next in this line is Giovanni (1457-1501) who was the nephew of Pope Sixtus IV and the brother of Pope Julius II. In 1474, his uncle made him Lord of Senigallia and Mondavio. Additionaly, he was Prefect of Rome, Duke of Sora and Arce. Pope Innocent VIII promoted him to Captain General of the Church. He led pro-French expeditions from 1494-1501. In 1495, he

Titian. Public domain. via Wikimedia Commons

conquered Ceprano, Monte Cassino and Terra Sancti Benedicti. Finally, 1496, he defended the Duchy against Prospero Colonna and Frederick IV of Naples.[5]

Gasparini, Public domain, via Wikimedia Commons

Della Scala

The Della Scala family is from Verona and has an obscure origin. It is believed that the family began with my 24th great-grandfather Balduino in the 12th century.

My 22nd great-grandfather was Alberto I (1241-1301). From 1272 to 1277, he was Podesta of Mantua. He became the Lord of Verona in 1277 after his elder brother Mastino was assassinated. He enacted strict laws to avenge his brother's death. He was married to Verde da Salizzole.[1]

Unidentified engraver, Public domain, via Wikimedia Commons

Their second son was Alboino (1284-1311). In January of 1298, his marriage was stipulated to Caterina Visconti, and celebrated in September. Around the same time, he became an armed knight in the Scaligera (Della Scala) military. In 1304, he became Lord of Verona and Podesta. From 1305-1310 he was actively involved in a number of diplomatic and military encounters. He had three children with Beatrice da Correggio, both sons became Lords of Verona, and his daughter became the abbess of a Veronese monastery.[2]

Next in my line was Mastino (1329-1351). He and his brother Alberto II ruled Verona. He abandoned his father's policy of peace and conquered Brescia, Parma and Lucca. This event led to the formation of a league against Verona, with Milan, Ferrara, Mantua and the Papal States as members. In 1338 he murdered his uncle Bartolomeo, the bishop of Verona. He was eventually surrounded by the league and lost all his territories except for Verona and Vicenza.

Mastino's daughter Beatrice Regina (1335-1384) was my 19th great-grandmother. She married Bernabo Visconti. She gave birth to fifteen children, five boys and ten girls. Her sons were Lords of Parma, Pavia and Bergamo.[3]

Andrea di Bonaiuto, Public domain, via Wikimedia Commons

Farnese

The origin of the Farnese family is unknown. Early documentation shows that they owned minor fiefdoms in the ninth century and were most likely from French or Lombard origins. The earliest document found from 1134 shows a Petrus De Farneto, who fought in Puglia against the Normans. It is certain that they ruled several fiefdoms around Orvieto and Viterbo. For about four centuries there were notable men with the names Ranuccio and Petrus alternating, but the exact succession is unclear.

The earliest Farnese ancestor that I have found is my 16th great-grandfather, Ranuccio (1400-1450). He escaped a massacre that threatened the entire family. He was a Senator of Rome in 1417 and Defender of the Papal State, supported by the Colonna family. His fame and authority grew under Pope Eugene IV. Ranuccio married Agnese Monaldeschi, who was from a very powerful family in Orvieto. The marriage of my 15th great-grandfather Pier Luigi (1435–1487) to Giovanella Caetani elevated the family into Roman aristocracy.

Pier Luigi's son Alessandro (1468-1549), my 14th great-grandfather, was the first cardinal in the family and later became Pope Paul III. His story is very interesting in that his sister Giulia Farnese was the mistress of Rodrigo Borgia (Pope Alexander VI). Pope Alexander elevated Alessandro to the position of Treasure of the Church. A year later, in 1492, he made him Cardinal. He was known as the "petticoat cardinal" due to his sister's relationship with the pope. This story is very prominent in "The Borgias" TV series.

Alessandro was not ordained a priest until 1519 and conducted himself like a Renaissance nobleman. He was a favored by Pope Leo X and constructed the Palazzo Farnese in Rome, now the French Embassy. He fathered four children with his mistress Sylvia Ruffini, who was from a wellborn Roman family. Pope Julius II anointed him Bishop of Parma in 1509, and in 1519, he ended his relationship with Sylvia Ruffini.

Cardinal Farnese (Alessandro) had excellent diplomatic skills and was invaluable to five popes, and in 1534 at the age of 67 he was elected Pope. His papacy was very interesting and there were many significant events that took place. The Jesuit order and Ursuline nuns were founded during his reign. He excommunicated Henry VIII, asserted papal control over central Italy, and curbed abuses in the Church.

Titian, Public domain, via Wikimedia Commons

In 1545, the Pope convened the Council of Trent, inaugurated by Cardinal Giovanni Del Monte, which hammered out decrees on the Scriptures, original sin, the sacraments, and reform of the Church. Dedicated to the arts, Paul III increased funding to the Vatican Library and brought back the University of Rome. He also contracted Michelangelo complete the fresco in the Sistine Chapel.

Pope Paul III's legacy is that as intelligent, obliging, and good-hearted. His tomb is in St. Peter's and is the work of Guglielmo Della Porta, a student of Michelangelo [1].

Pope Paul's son Pier Luigi I (1503-1547) was the Duke of Parma and Piacenza. He was known to be violent and impulsive and was often at odds with the Papacy (he participated in the Sack of Rome) until his father ascended to the throne. He then became a Standard Bearer for the Church, Duke of Castro, and Marquis of Novara. It was his father who granted him Parma and Piacenza in 1545. He was a good administrator and a reformer who distrusted the imperial government. He married Geronima Orsini[2].

My entry into this family was through Pier Luigi's daughter Vittoria Farnese (1519-1602). Vittoria was an important pawn in the family's marriage strategies and was proposed by her grandfather (the pope) and two cardinal brothers (Pope Paul III elevated his two teenage grandsons to Cardinal) to marry into the Medici, Colonna, and other noble Italian families. In 1539, she was also proposed to King Charles V of France after the death of his wife.

At the ripe old age of twenty-eight, she was proposed to Guidobaldo Della Rovere, the Duke of Urbino. This union was good for the duke as she was the granddaughter of the reigning pope. It was also good for the pope to have the duke of an extremely important territory on his side. Vittoria's dowry consisted of 60,000 Ducati as well as the equivalent of 20,000 Ducati in jewels, gold, and silver.

Upon her arrival in Urbino, she had her brother-in-law elevated to cardinal and had investiture of the ducal territory in perpetuity to Guidobaldo and his male descendants. She was very skilled in governing, apparently much better than Guidobaldo. In her later years, she had several disputes with her son Francesco Maria to the extent that she left the duchy in 1584, only to return in 1588.

Titian, Public domain, via Wikimedia Commons

Giacomo Vighi, Public domain, via Wikimedia Commons

Filangieri

The Filangieri family is another ancient family from Naples, dating back to my great-grandfather, Angerio, who was 28 years old. The name comes from the sons of Guglielmo, "Filii Angerii." The family was a large part of history under the Norman and Swabian rule. They held many lordships and military titles and were dignitaries of the church. They held the Order of Malta, Golden Fleece, and other orders of chivalry. It is believed by some that Angerio was a Norman soldier who arrived in Italy after Robert Guiscard. Angerio is buried in the Benedictine Church of St. Trinta Di Cave and is most likely from the Lords of Arnes and the lineage of Rollo, the Duke of Normandy. [1]

My 24th great-grandfather, Riccardo, is the first in this line to have any real prominence. He was the Marshal of the Court of Frederick II. He participated in the Fifth Crusade, commanding 500 knights. He was appointed Governor of Jerusalem but held the position for only a few days. In 1231, he went back to the Holy Land with the Office of Imperiale Legate for the Kingdom of Jerusalem. His son, Aldoino started the Counts of Avellino line. He participated in the war against the Palaeologus of Byzantium in 1277 and was Justice of Bari until 1284. He was later the Master of the Royal Court.

Giacomo was my 20th great-grandfather in this line, and he was aligned with Charles III of Sicily and presumably the executioner of Basilicata. He was invested with Avellino (as the first Count) in 1382, after it had been confiscated from the Del Balzo family. With royal assent, in 1382, he bought the fief of Montemarano and the Castle of Tito. He was also invested with the fief of Petraperciata in the same year. In 1392, he was the Marshal of the Kingdom of Sicily. His son, Giacomo Nicola was the second Count of Avellino and defended it from King Ladislao I of Sicily.

There is an interesting story about Giacomo Nicola's daughter Caterina, who married Giovanni Sergianni Caracciolo, which is where I enter this family:

She was Lady of Chiusano, Santo Mango, Civello, Frigento, Orta, and other fiefdoms from 1418. On the death of her brother Giacomo Nicola, who did not have any descendants, King Ladislao I of Sicily made the family assets fall back to the Regio Fisco, ignoring the claims of Filippo Filangieri. Ladislao sold or gave the assets away, with the privilege so the new owners would not be harassed. Years later, the new sovereign Giovanna II authorized the marriage of Caterina Filangieri to her favorite, Sergianni Caracciolo. The royal decision to authorize the female succession resulted in a violent quarrel between Caterina on the one hand, and her uncle Filippo and cousin Matteo Riccardo on the other. Giovanna II then proposed to settle the question in the legal seat by setting up a commission chaired by the Grand Chancellor of the Kingdom, Marino Boffa. The commission, made up of magistrates loyal to the will of the sovereign and purposely educated, was in favor of Caterina Filangieri. (Amongst other things, Marino Boffa was one of the many lovers of Giovanna II and Guerello Caracciolo was a relative of Segianni.)

Leaving aside the distinction between bourgeois and feudal assets that were accumulated as a whole, the following was established: 1) Female succession in the absence of male heirs, excluding uncles; 2) For those who followed the jure francorum, the sister was excluded from the succession if she had inherited assets from her brother; 3) For those who followed the jure langobardorum, the sister succeeded if she was endowed with goods by her father.

From this, it was deduced that Catherine succeeded in the dynastic fiefdoms, having received 800 ounces of dowry from her father to be paid in the family "goods." The resolution was enacted in the form of a law with the name of Prammatica Filangeria in Castelnuovo di Napoli on January 19, 1418. Queen Giovanna II, confirmed on October 12, 1418, allowed Caterina Filangieri to sue the owners of the family assets granted by King Ladislao I, and forced them to return the assets. The Prammatica Filangeria was mentioned by Prince Gaetano Filangieri in his famous political essay, "The Science of Legislation" (1780-1783) as a prototype of legislative abuse related to succession. After the murder of her husband, Caterina underwent the confiscation of Avellino and other minor fiefs on August 29, 1432. [2]

Gonzaga

The Gonzaga family was an Italian dynasty that ruled Mantua from 1328 to 1707. They also ruled Montferrat and Casale from 1536 to 1707. The early history is uncertain, but by the 12th century the Corradi family of Gonzaga were established feudal lords. They took their name from the village and castle of Gonzaga. The first prominent member was my 20th great-grandfather Ludovico.[1]

While it is unclear, it is believed that the ancient line goes back to my 25th great-grandfather Filippo (1125-1195). Antonio my 22nd, great-grandfather, was an elder of the people in 1259, but banished and confined in 1273. He was rich and influential in Mantua and owned assets in Gonzaga. Note: His succession is not verified at this time. It is believed that he is Ludovico's grandfather.[2]

Unknown person, Public domain, via Wikimedia Commons

Ludovico I (1268-1360) was a very rich patrician from Mantua. He was Podesta of Modena in 1313, Podesta of Mantua in 1318 and Podesta of Parma in 1319. He was Captain General of Mantua in 1328 and Imperial Vicar in 1329 and 1340. He was also Lord on Reggio Emilia beginning in 1335 and Lord over six other fiefdoms at the same time. I descend from his first wife, Richlide Ramberti.

Ludovico's son Guido (1290-1369) was the second Lord of Mantua. It is not clear who his mother was and there is no history of his early years. It is known, that in 1328, he participated in the coup d'etat, which overthrew the Bonacolsian lordship over Mantua. As the eldest son, he represented his father in many significant agreements especially those pertaining to the rights to the Bonacolsian assets. He was made Captain of the People when his father died in 1360.[3]

I descend from two of his children. The second son Ludovico II (1334-1382) who became Captain General when his father passed away.

In 1362, in a plot to gain power, he killed his elder brother. [4] He was eventually forgiven by his father. He was married to Alda d'Este the daughter of Obizzo III Marquis of d'Este and Lord of Ferrara. Their son, Francesco (1366-1407) was Captain General from 1388. He was later named Imperial Vicar and regained several cities from the Della Scala. As Captain General for the Duke of Milan in 1401, he conquered Isola and Rodolesco in 1404, Peschiera in 1405 and Lonato in 1406. He was married twice, and after accusing his first

Unidentified engraver, Public domain, via Wikimedia Commons

wife, Agnese Visconti of adultery, he had her beheaded. His second wife was Margherita Malatesta, the daughter of the Lord Rimini.

Ugolino distinguished himself in the wars against the Visconti. He was married three times, his second wife was Emilia della Gherardesca. Their daughter, Teodora was my 18th great-grandmother and she married Federico Paolo da Montefeltro.

Francesco's son, Gianfrancesco (1395-1444) was Captain General of Mantua from 1407, with a guardian. He was the first Marquis of Mantua with Imperial Diploma. He fought for the pope in 1412 and for the Malatesta in 1417. From 1432-1437 he was Captain General of Venetian Arms. He was lord of over a dozen fiefdoms. He married Paola Malatesta, the daughter of Malatesta V Lord of Pesaro.

Gianfrancesco's son Ludovico III (1414-1478) was my 15th great-grandfather. He was known as "the Turk" and was disinherited by his father for siding with the Venetians against the Duke of Milan. He was later forgiven and reinstated in 1440. He was the second Duke of

Mantua Lieutenant General of the Duke of Milan in 1470. He was married to Barbara of Brandenburg daughter of Margrave John IV and Barbara Duchess of Saxony.[5]

Next in line was Federico "the hunchback" (1442-1484) he was the third Marquis of Mantua and assumed power in 1478. As a General for the Duchy of Milan he took part in the war following the Pazzi conspiracy. At the instigation of Pope Sixtus IV, he attacked Lugano and in 1479 fought in Tuscany. In 1482, he fought with the Duke of Ferrara against the Venetians and the pope. In 1484, he had to hand over Asola as part of a peace agreement and was so disappointed he died in July of that year. He married Margarita Duchess of Bavaria the daughter of Duke Albert II and Anna Duchess of Brunswick-Grubenhagen.[6]

Unknown person, Public domain, via Wikimedia Commons

Perhaps my favorite Gonzaga great-grandfather is Francesco II (1466-1519). He was married to perhaps the woman of the Renaissance,

Kunsthistorisches Museum, Public domain, via Wikimedia Commons

Isabella d'Este. In 1469, he was named an armed knight by Emperor Frederick III. In 1484, when his father died, he took over as the fourth marquis. He encouraged the improvement of agriculture and the cultivation of abandoned fields. He also oversaw an accurate census, in 1484, that showed a population of 128,000 inhabitants, with 32,000 in the capital, with and income estimated at 122,000 gold scudi. He also scaled down the court and household.

His wedding to Isabella was celebrated in Mantua on February 15th, 1490 and was lavish and prestigious. The couple could not be more different. He was coarse in features, sensual in temperament and greedy for pleasures (he had many extramarital affairs). He was a lover of horses and merry-go-rounds. He was not very cultured but sensitive to the flattery of writers. Isabella, on the other hand, was beautiful intelligent and elegant. He had six children with Isabella and at least three "natural" daughters.

In 1495, he was appointed commander of an army, to go against Charles VIII consisting of 2,500 lancers, 8,000 infantry and 2,000 soldiers, with payment of 44,000 gold scudi. Over the course of the next year, he won many victories and was rewarded with bonuses of money and property and welcomed with honors. In March of 1496, he visits Pope Alexander in Rome and is given a golden rose. He meets with Cesare Borgia and pays homage to his sister Lucrezia (apparently over the years he did a lot more with her). He also meets with Ferdinand II the King of Naples and holds a war council. In May he moved on Lucera and defeated the French garrison. That summer, he contracted typhoid and decides to return to Mantua. During the trip, he contracts malaria, but eventually reunites with Isabella.

Kunsthistorisches Museum, Public domain, via Wikimedia Commons

In 1497, he loses his contract with Venice and with it, 44,000 Ducati per year. He is able to replace this with a contract with Ludovico il Moro in 1498 for 40,000 Ducati. In 1501, he is appointed Captain General of the Imperial Army in Italy. At this time, he had fears that he would be captured at the wedding of his brother-in-law to Lucrezia Borgia. In 1503, he was supposed to go to Naples to participate in military action against Spain, but he became ill and returned to Mantua.

Unknown Person, Public domain, via Wikimedia Commons

In 1506, he is appointed lieutenant general of the papal army by Pope Julius II and directs the capture of Bologna. For the next ten years or so, he wages various battles and skirmishes throughout the Italian peninsula. His health steadily declines, and he dies with Isabella by his side on March 29, 1519.[7]

As told in Love-in-the-Renaissance-The-Secret-Story-between-Lucrezia-Borgia-and-Francesco-Gonzaga

"The love story between Lucrezia Borgia, the natural daughter of the pope Alexander VI (Rodrigo Borgia), and Francesco Gonzaga seems

to come out from the pages of War and Peace. The pair met only three or may be four times, but they gave life to a secret correspondence in the years between 1507 and 1513. In the background, the disagreement between the two families and the bloody battles of the War of Italy, when France, Venice and the Papacy competed for the supremacy in Northern Italy.

Lucrezia Borgia had arrived to the court of Ferrara in 1502. She had married the Duke Alfonso d Este, after two other marriages ended badly, or very badly. The Borgia were one of the most powerful families in Italy at that time, feared because of the intrigues of the pope Alexander VI and his son Cesare, brother to Lucrezia, the bloodthirsty conqueror of the Romagna who is thought to have inspired Machiavelli s Prince. The sister of the Duke Alfonso, Isabella d Este, had married Francesco II Gonzaga, to strengthen a traditional alliance between the two families.

The Marquis of Mantua Francesco Gonzaga comes to Ferrara in 1504, to meet his new sister-in-law Lucrezia, since he had not been able to take part in the wedding banquet in 1502. Lucrezia s father, pope Alexander VI, had died in 1503. Pope Julius II, archenemy to the Borgia, had imprisoned Lucrezia s brother Cesare, who had conquered the government of the Romagna with the support of his father. The power of the Borgia was suddenly declining. Francesco had a generous and impetuous character, seasoned with a pinch of ingenuity. Instinctively, he finds the most direct route to Lucrezia s hearth: he promises to intercede for the release of Cesare Borgia. Really, he is promising something greater than him, that he is not in the power to obtain, but Lucrezia knows that the Este do not love her family. She sees Francesco as the unique person who can try something to help her brother.

In 1507 Francesco was appointed general captain of the papal army. During the festivities of the Carnival, he arrives at the court of Ferrara proud of his new title. It is now the time of Lucrezia to welcome him. The whole Ferrara can see the affection she shows towards Francesco. Lucrezia throws herself in dancing and drags him whit her. She dances and dances with a so great fervour, that she loses the child she had in womb. The Duke Alfonso receives the news badly. Once again, he is not able to see an heir to the Duchy. He considers his wife responsible of what has happened and does nothing to hide this sentiment.

Ercole-Zilio writes to Francesco: She (Lucrezia) loves you very very much and much more than you think...." It is not known if Lucrezia and Francesco met at one of their summer residences (Borgoforte, Belriguardo, Reggio Emilia) in 1507. What is known, is that Lucrezia gives birth to a child, Ercole II, in the April of 1508. Here is the so long desired heir of the Duchy. Alfonso, the Duke, was away: he did not want to assist to another death. Destiny wanted that they die in the same year, 1519, a few months one after the other. Francesco in March, due to his syphilis, Lucrezia in June after another pregnancy. She had given Alfonso seven children." [8]

Francesco's and Isabella's daughter Eleonora Violanta (1493-1550) was my 13th great-grandmother and she married Francesco Maria Della Rovere I the Duke of Urbino. Their son Federico (1500-1540) was my 12th great-grandfather.

Federico II (1500-1540) was the Duke of Mantua and the Marquis of Monferrato. He was held hostage by Pope Julius II in 1510 and by Francesco I King of France in 1515. He was Captain General of the Church in 1521 and fought in Parma and Milan. He was originally contracted to marry Maria Palaiologos, but this was voided by Pope Clement in exchange for two prisoners. He then was contracted to Charles V's cousin, Julia of Aragon, but later paid 50,000 Ducati to have the contract voided. He pushed the pope to restore his original contract to Maria, but when she died, he married her sister Margherita. They had seven children together. As a patron of the arts, he commissioned both Titian and Raphael to paint his portrait. Like his father, he suffered from syphilis. [9] [10]

Titian, Public domain, via Wikimedia Commons

Federico's daughter Isabella Gonzaga (1537-1579) was my 11th great-grandmother and was married to Ferrante Francesco d'Avalos d'Aquino Prince of Francavilla.

Titian, Public domain, via Wikimedia Commons

Valentin Carderera y Solano, Public domain, via Wikimedia Commons

Malatesta

The Malatesta originated in Rimini with Malatesta, a rich land-owner from Montefeltro. They are first mentioned in a land purchase deed from 1136. Early in the families' history, they supported the Guelphs. Malatesta I was Mayor of Rimini, and his son Malatesta II da Verucchio held dominance over other lands in Romagna and Marche.[1]

Malatesta da Verucchio was my 20th great-grandfather. He was the leader of the Guelphs in Romagna and became Podesta of Rimini in 1239. In 1295, he killed off the leaders of the Ghibelline family, Parcitati and became the undisputed leader of Rimini. [2]

His son, Pandolfo I (d 1326) was Lord of Rimini and Pesaro but had little skill in defending them from enemies. He did however defeat the Montefeltro and Uberto Malatesta that earned him a knighthood from the pope.[3]

Pandolfo's son, Galeotto (1299-1385) seized power over Rimini in 1334 with Antico Malatesta and they were proclaimed after inviting his cousins into the city and having them imprisoned. In 1335, the brothers were in a protracted war with Ferrantino Novello and the Montefeltro's until 1343. In the mid-fifteenth century, the brothers consolidated power and controlled Ancona, Osimo, Iesi, Cingoli and Ascoli. In 1352, they led a campaign in Abruzzo for Louis Anjou King of Sicily.

In 1354, the pope summoned the two to the Curia, they were excommunicated in Dec of 1354 for failing to appear. In 1355, King Louis tried to intervene with the pope on their behalf to no avail, and they were imprisoned by the papal forces. Later that year, they were released, relieved of their excommunication and made vicar generals of the Church.

In 1363, he took command of the Florentine army and defeated Pisa. In 1368, Pope Urban V made him a Senator of Rome. Pope Gregory XI sent him to Modena to help Niccolo d'Este who was attacked by

Manfredino Saluzzo. He acquired in 1371 for 17,000 Ducati and in 1378, the pope appointed him governor of Cessna. Despite his age, he assumed command of military operations in Umbria and Tuscany in 1384.[4]

Next in line was Andrea (1373-1416) my 15th great-grandfather. He inherited Cessna, Roncofreddo, Fossombrone and Galeotto Novello when his father died. In 1403, he aided Cardinal Baldassarre Cossa (later the anti-pope John XXIII) in the conquest of Romagna and the capture of a series of castles in the Apennine Valley. In 1409, he married his third wife, Polissena di San Severino, a relative of the King of Naples, giving him a military contract with Naples. [5]

Galeotto's daughter Margherita (1371-1399) was my 17th great-grandmother. She married Francesco Gonzaga I who ruled Mantua.

Another entry into this line was Paola Malatesta (1339-1449) my 16th, great-grandmother. She married Gianfrancesco Gonzaga in 1409. This event was the third union between these two powerful families, and she brought a dowry of 5,000 gold florins, however, it is unclear if that was ever paid. She enjoyed the wealth of Mantua including jewels' chests and various personal articles from her mother-in-law. She was known to be responsible, attentive and more stolid than her husband. Paola was also known to be very religious and sensitive. She obtained from the pope the right to build churches, convents and monasteries in Mantua, Milan and Piacenza.[6]

Apparently, Paola's brother Galeazzo (1385-1461) did not have the fortitude that his sister had. He lacked courage, military, and political skills. In 1416, he was captured and imprisoned by the Perugian leader Braccioda Monte and was ransomed for 30,000 scudi. He was imprisoned again, in 1424 with his wife, when the castle of Gradara was conquered by the Lombard militias. When his father died, he and his brothers took over Pesaro, Fossombrone and Senigallia, which the eventually lost. In 1432, the brothers were able to re-acquire much of what was lost. Galeazzo's daughter, Elisabetta (1407 - 1477) was my 17th great-grandmother. [7]

The father of Paola and Galeazzo was Malatesta IV (1370-1429) known as "dei sonetti" (of the Sonnets) as he loved the culture and art. He married Elisabetta da Varano and between them they had seven children. In 1385, he became Lord of Pesaro when Pope Urban VI contracted him to wage war against Clement VII, the anti-pope. Five years later, he battled with Bologna and soon after fought against Milan. In 1394, the antipope, Benedict XIII, named him Captain General of Bologna to fight against Boniface VIII. In 1404, he contracted with Venice, and was given 20,000 troops to fight Padua. He sided with Alexander V in 1409 and fought with Florence in a war against Naples. Florence hired Malatesta in 1423, to fight against Milan. [8]

Montefeltro

The Montefeltro family is a branch of the of the Counts of Carpegna to which Buonconte belonged who became the lord of Urbino in 1234. From the late 14th century to the early part of the 15th the lordship of the Montefeltro's had the recognition of the Church. Oddantonio had the title of Duke of Urbino from Pope Eugene IV (1443). His brother Federico was a famous leader and patron. On his death, he was succeeded by his son Guidobaldo (1472-1508), who temporarily lost the duchy due to the attack of Cesare Borgia. Reinstated to possession by Pope Julius II, he died prematurely of illness and the dominion of the Montefeltro passed to the della Rovere.[1]

My 21st great-grandfather was Guido (d 1298) a man of arms, and senator of Rome. A tenacious Ghibelline, he fought against Sienna in 1271, beat the Bolognese and the Guelphs in 1275, and took an active part in the struggles of Romagna. As captain of the people and mayor of Pisa, he defended the city victoriously from Florence. Back in Romagna he then took possession of Urbino in 1292. In 1295 he entered the Franciscan order. Admired by his contemporaries, including Dante for his military prowess, he was also judged an astute politician.[2]

My 20th great-grandfather Federico (d 1322) was the son Guido and brother of Bonconte, he succeeded his father and uncle Galasso as the leader Ghibellinism in the Marche region, without the same success. After being expelled from Cesena of which he was captain of the people (1301), he preferred to carry out his action in the Umbria-Marche area, dominating the political scene for about twenty years and was at the head of the societas Ghibellinorum della Marca, then Captain of Osimo and Iesi (1309) and mayor of Pisa (1310). Amongst the most faithful supporters of Henry VII, whom he welcomed in Pisa (1312) and with whom he was at the siege of Florence. He was present at his death, in September 1313, he wrote to Cardinal Niccolò da Prato in defense of Fra 'Bernardino da Montepulciano, accused of having poisoned the emperor. Back in the Marca, he resumed his anti-Guelph action, occupying Recanati and pushing Osimo and Spoleto to rise up against the papal vicar, for which John XXII, after having excommunicated him along with other rectors of Marche cities, "finding them, in several articles of resia, and such in idolatry" (Villani IX 141), he launched a crusade against them (1322). While he was in Urbino to gather men, the citizens rose up, because of "a large size, or taxation of money" (ibid.), And killed him along with his son (25 April 1322).[3]

Nolfo da Montefeltro (1295-1363) was the son of Federico. In 1322, he escaped the massacre in which his father and brother lost their lives, perhaps fleeing to San Marino together with his second cousin Speranza (whose common ancestor was Montefeltrano di Montefeltro). With his cousin, some other relatives and the Tarlati of Pietramala, and after a first unsuccessful attempt, in April 1324, he recovered the city and the countryside of Urbino. In August of 1324, under his command, eight hundred knights and four thousand infantry, surrounded Castel Cavallino near Urbino he fought a bloody battle that ended with the massacre of those who had participated in the Urbino insurrection and who had been responsible for the death of his father and brother.

In 1326-1327 he was mayor of Fabriano, at the time, a city that was the enemy of the Church, which he defended from the Malatesta assault. At the beginning of 1327, all the cities of the Marca, except Ancona, rebelled against the pontiff and adhered to the league led by the Montefeltro. Nolfo supported the emperor Ludwig of Bavaria during his descent into Italy and on 27 March 1328 he received along with Galasso a diploma confirming the dominion of numerous castles and villas located in Montefeltro. Two days later, the emperor granted them the faculty to create judges and notaries and to legitimize bastards and with a second privilege divided between Speranza on the one hand and Nolfo with his brothers on the other, the possessions and rights of imperial origin that already they had belonged to their relative Galasso, who died childless in 1300. But with a further privilege issued on 27 March the emperor confirmed full possession of his ancient comitatus to the city of Urbino, thus recognizing the Montefeltro as counts of Urbino.

After the death of Castruccio Castracani degli Antelminelli (3 September 1328), the emperor appointed Nolfo as vicar of Pistoia, hoping to contain the Florentine power. As soon as Ludovico il Bavaro left Italy in April 1329, the cities of the Marche gathered to agree on a way to return to the obedience of the Church. In September 1330, the assets of the Counts of Montefeltro appeared to have been confiscated by the Apostolic Chamber, in that same year Nolfo swore allegiance to King

John of Bohemia, son of Henry VII, who also went to Italy, and appointed him councilor on April 9, 1333. Nolfo was able to reconcile with the pope, bringing with him also several Marche cities which, with Urbino, were acquitted by ecclesiastical censures (August 1333). This event happened, however, in a period in which the Malatesta had passed in an absolute majority to the side opposing the Papacy and in a period in which the legate, defeated at Ferrara along with the king of Bohemia, was losing power day by day. Bringing with it also several cities of the Marches which, with Urbino, were acquitted by ecclesiastical censures (August 1333).

Despite the enormous power of the Malatesta, whose domination went as far as Ascoli and Jesi and allowed them to control much of the coastal strip between Romagna and Marche, the counts of Montefeltro had managed to consolidate their dominion in the geographic area that, traditionally, had been at the center of their strategic interests for a century and a half, while also maintaining a prestige that far exceeded the borders of the directly controlled territory, as evidenced by the numerous magistracies exercised in the cities of central Italy.

Nolfo's actions, aimed at the recovery of the territory located in the present northern Marche, did not go further. Some pontifical letters of the thirties and forties of the century inform us of the subtraction of some castles from the Roman and Ravenna churches but overall, until 1348 the good relationship of the counts of Montefeltro with the Papacy persisted, which had converging interests above all in facing domination Malatesta.

In 1341, Nolfo found himself again on the anti-Florentine side, joining the league of Luchino Visconti, lord of Milan. In charge of the command of the Pisan foeditores, on 12 October, he defeated the army of Florence and on 17 June 1342 he participated in the occupation of Lucca. Recognized as a skilled man of war, in 1344, he commanded the Venetian army against the Count of Gorizia. Successful winner, on 19 September he was ascribed along with his brothers to the Venetian citizenship.

In 1348, while King Louis of Hungary was in Italy to avenge the killing of his brother Andrea and to reclaim the throne of Sicily, Nolfo became a part of the vast pro-Hungarian alliance (and thus anti-Neapolitan and anti-papal) that had gathered around Giovanni Visconti, archbishop of Milan, being placed in charge of operations in central Italy. He besieged Cantiano, in 1351, he took part in the military campaign that was being fought in Tuscany and during the following winter he took possession of the upper Valtiberina, was defeated in Orvieto and repaired in Sansepolcro, whence he moved to take Bettona in August 1352. Having exhausted the propulsive thrust of the Visconti war, which had not brought appreciable results.

At the time of Cardinal Egidio Albornoz's descent into Italy in 1354, Nolfo and his brothers, fully invested in the recovery campaign that the legate carried out effectively, were among the first to come to terms. After being exhorted to return the lands unduly occupied to the detriment of the Church and after having tried to obtain mediation from the Emperor Charles IV, to whose family they had been linked for decades, Nolfo and Enrico went to Gubbio and on 20 June 1355, they declared themselves guilty, they swore allegiance to the legate and asked to be acquitted by submitting an act; on 8 July the city of Urbino did the same. On 26 July Nolfo, Enrico and Feltrano and the representatives of the Municipalities of Cagli and Urbino signed solemn pacts with the legate. The fidelity of the counts and the cities to the Roman Church was reaffirmed; compromising agreements were stipulated for the choice of Podestà in Urbino and Cagli; procedures were started to readmit some exiles; the counts and communities were acquitted of ecclesiastical censures and were returned to their state; the accounts were finally returned to the civitatis custody of Urbino, Cagli and other cities and lands, with the temporary exception of San Marino, waiting for the Malatesta to submit, while the countryside was returned to the city of Urbino with the promise of being able to freely elect the podestà and to exercise the mere and mixed empire.

In 1358, Nolfo was called by the Sienese to direct military operations against the Perugini, but he did not accept the job. In 1360, he participated in the capture of Bologna under the orders of Albornoz. The last years of his life were marked by a phase of less political weight of the Montefeltro family, which, held back by the presence of the legate, appeared less able to maintain a solid network of clienteles with the other noble families of the region.[4]

My 17th great-grandfather Antonio da Montefeltro (1348-1404) by Federico Novello di Nolfo. Litta believes his mother was Teodora (Tora) d'Ugolino Gonzaga, who was the wife of her uncle Paolo di Montefeltro, son of Galasso. On 30 September 1363, Cardinal Egidio Albornoz conferred the civitatis custody of Urbino on Paolo, who received it on his own and as the tutor of Antonio and of the other nephews Nolfo, Guido and Galasso, all still minors.

In the autumn of 1367, Antonio married Agnesina Dei Prefetti di Vico, who, especially in the years between the fourteenth and fifteenth centuries, had prominence in the management of the affairs of the Urbino state during the long absences of her husband and the minority of her eldest son Guidantonio. The couple had at least two daughters: Battista (1384-1448), wife of Galeazzo Malatesta, lord of Pesaro, and Anna (d. 1434), wife of Galeotto Belfiore Malatesta.

Agnesina was the daughter of Giovanni (III) Di Vico (d. 1366), who had been the most powerful lord of Tuscia and who was a bitter enemy of the legate. The convergence of interests determined by this kinship (some descendants of the Prefects of Vico later took root in Montefeltro, becoming lords of the castles of Casteldelci, Faggiola and Senatello) favored an alliance against the pontiff, which materialized in the summer of 1369, when the young Antonio, who served in the service of the legate against Perugia, abandoned the papal army and placed himself in command of the rebels along with his brothers and brothers-in-law.

In that summer of 1369, Antonio managed to bring his own militias to the walls of Viterbo, then the residence of Pope Urban V. Having solid points of support in the Apennine area, in the Valtiberina and in the Montefeltro (where he kept the two fearsome fortresses of Pietrarubbia and Pietramaura), Antonio tried to take Urbino, which, after being occupied by Pandolfo Malatesta, was now firmly in the hands of Cardinal Grimoard, but was unable to do so. The following year (winter 1370), he went to Avignon along with his brothers and obtained from the new Pope Gregory XI the rights to Urbino and a commission of 100 florins a month, despite the opposition of Cardinal Grimoard, who describes him in harsh terms in his connection to Cardinal d'Estaing.

Another opportunity to return to Urbino arose at the beginning of 1374, when the rector of Urbino and Massa Trabaria Filippo Corsini managed to foil a conspiracy in which Antonio and his brothers were probably involved. Shortly after the so-called war of the Eight Saints between the Florentine Republic and the Papacy determined the formation of a five-year alliance between Florence and Milan and fomented the rebellions which, spreading throughout the Papal State, from Viterbo to Ravenna, led almost everywhere to expulsion of ecclesiastical rectors. Antonio having shown that he wanted to become a "son" of the Florentine municipality and Gubbio and Città di Castello had already risen, in December 1375 the Florentines supported the uprising of Massa Trabaria (which since then would cease to exist as a province) and, immediately afterwards, that of Urbino. Galeotto Malatesta ran with his men to strengthen the defense of the fortress, but on December 24th Antonio, who had moved from Città di Castello with 400 horses, managed to enter Urbino and was acclaimed lord. Galeotto Malatesta took refuge in Cagli, but after a few days he was also expelled from that city, which gave himself over to Montefeltro, who strengthened his domain immediately reaching an agreement with the Gabriellis of Gubbio and subsequently contracting a marriage between his brother Nolfo and Margherita's daughter of Cante Gabrielli.

After having resisted and counterattacked the Malatesta and after having kept up with the advance of the companies of the "Bretons" of Cardinal Robert of Geneva (later antipope Clement VII) sent by Gregory XI, Antonio was able to further consolidate the results achieved. In October-November 1377, Francesco dei Prefetti reconciled with the pontiff, who had every interest, having in the meantime returned to Rome from Avignon, to find support in central Italy.

Alongside the achievement of the apostolic vicariate and the stipulation of a truce with Galeotto Malatesta (21 March 1380) which was interrupted by the frequent resumption of hostilities, the major work of construction and consolidation of the domain was the assumption of protection and then of the lordship of the city of Gubbio, for years troubled by internal struggles in which Antonio had long supported the opposing faction to the Gabriellis. On March 24th he occupied the city with 2000 infantry and 800 horses. A solemn peace followed (November 7, 1384) with Galeotto Malatesta, obtained with the mediation of Gian Galeazzo Visconti, lord of Milan, with whom Antonio in the following would strengthen the alliance more and more.

The years that followed saw Antonio work a progressive consolidation of the state, favored in this also by the death of the lord of Rimini and the fragmentation of the Malatesta possessions that followed. In October 1385, he managed to temporarily occupy the domain that Francesco Gabrielli, who had escaped from Gubbio, had built in Cantiano, thus pushing Florence, as well as the Malatestas, to the offensive against him. After various episodes of war and an attempt to raze Gubbio, the Florentines managed to negotiate a favorable peace for them, which was signed on the following 18 July. The count declared himself recommended by the Republic, returned Cantiano to the Gabriellis and allowed him to be elected in Gubbio, a mayor of Florentine citizenship, while maintaining control of the city. A few years later (1394).

On 17 November 1388 a new peace was stipulated between Antonio di Montefeltro and the Malatesta, again with the mediation of Gian Galeazzo Visconti. Antonio became a soldier and adherent, remaining so until his death, holding positions of prestige and being a part of the noble procession of those who, in 1395, greeted him Duke of Milan.

The passage to the Visconti alliance distanced him from Florence and on May 20, 1392, he issued new rules for the choice of the podestà of Gubbio, whose main requirements now had to be no longer Florentine citizenship, but the liking of the lord and the title of doctor of law. Siding again against the Florentines and the Malatesta alongside the lord of Milan, he was for a long time engaged in war actions, with mixed results, until the peace (13 October 1393) which, wanted by the pope and supported by Gian Galeazzo Visconti, allowed the maintenance a decades-long understanding, and a balanced position between the two Montefeltro and Malatesta families; in the years immediately following, it was also strengthened by two crossed marriages, respectively between Guidantonio and Anna, sons of Antonio, and Rengarda and Galeotto Belfiore Malatesta, sons of Galeotto I.

In the years 1395-98, he fought against the anti-Discontean league, gathering around him the forces of various lords of central Italy. Included in the Venice truce of July-August 1398 (not without complaints from Florence, who did not want to understand him as he considered him a recommended one who fell into felony), he was about to become a lieutenant of the Duke of Milan and had already gone to Pavia, after leaving his wife Agnesina and son Guidantonio to govern the state, when, in September 1398, he fell ill with the plague. Having escaped death and went to the thermal baths of Petriolo in the Ombrone Valley to recover, he worked to ensure that Siena, with which he had long had friendly relations, would submit to the Duke of Milan. On 29 June 1399, he swore allegiance to the duke and became head of his secret council.

Antonio, having returned to Urbino in 1403, died there on 29 April 1404. On May 14th he was buried in the cloister of San Francesco, where in 1416, his wife Agnesina was also buried, whose sarcophagus is kept inside the church.

Antonio surrounded himself with a court of artists and writers, including Simone Serdini known as il Saviozzo. He ordered impressive works of architecture in Urbino, where he had a palace built, documented since 1392, which however does not correspond, as has long been believed to the current Palazzo Bonaventura seat of the University. The coats of arms that today surmounts the entrance portal of this building, which were believed to be those of Antonio and his wife Agnesina, are instead a few decades later. Antonio showed interest in poetry, so much so that he was the author himself.[5]

My 15th great-grandfather from this family was Federico Maria Montefelto (1422-1482). During his lifetime, he was Captain General for the Papal States, Milan, and Naples. He was the Duke of Urbino, Count of Montefelto, Urbino and Castel Durante, as well as the lord of many other fiefdoms.

He began his career at sixteen and conquered the castle of St. Leo. In 1444, his half-brother was assassinated, and he seized Urbino.

He was in the service of Florence until 1450, when Francesco Sforza, the Duke of Milan hired him (Federico never fought for free). However, after having his right eye put out in a tournament, he could not perform his duties. In 1451, he accepted a proposal from Alfonso V King of Naples, to battle against Florence. Federico's life was an inspiration for Machiavelli to write "Il Principe." To improve his field of vision, he had the bridge of his nose and an eyelid removed. This made him less vulnerable to sneak attacks on his person and allowed him to operate as a field commander, once again.

*P*iero della Francesca, Public domain, via Wikimedia Commons

Pope Pius II made him Gonfaloniere of the Holy Roman Church in 1458 and in 1464 Pope Paul II hired him to fight in the north. In 1467, he participated in the Battle of Molinella and in 1469 he defeated the Papal forces in a decisive battle. His daughter Giovanna married the nephew of Pope Sixtus IV and the Pope promoted him to Duke of Urbino in 1474.

He was married twice, and his second wife Battista Sforza is my 15th great-grandmother. Their daughter, Giovanna married Giovanni Della Rovere.[6]

Montferrat

The Montferrat were an Italian noble family and were a branch of the House of Palaiologos. It was founded by Teodoro the fourth son of Andronikos II the Byzantine Emperor. He inherited Monteferrat from his mother Yolande. He was chosen to go to Italy and converted to Roman Catholicism. [1]

Teodoro (1292-1338) was my 18th great-grandfather. He sailed to Genoa in 1306 and the following year married Argentina Spinola, daughter of Opicino Spinola the co-ruler of Genoa.[2] His son Giovanni (1321-1372) extended the boundaries of the margraviate with his cousins help Otto of Brunswick-Grubenhagen. He extended his holdings further, when Robert, King of Naples died in 1343. By 1344, he conquered Alessandria, Asti, Tortona, Bra and Alba. In 1355, he was given the cities of Cherasco, Novara and Pavia. He married the last titular Queen of Majorca Isabella.[3]

Teodoro II (1364-1418) was the third son of Giovanni and Isabella. When his brother Giovanni died in 1381, he took over the government at seventeen under the protection of Gian Galeazzo Visconti. In 1384, he requested confirmation from Wenceslaus IV. Teodoro accepted an invitation to marry Joan of Lorraine in 1393, she was the daughter of the Duke of Bar. In 1394, a conspiracy was revealed that would have poisoned his entire family, allegedly from ongoing hostilities with Achaia. Hostilities resumed in 1396 and continued through 1401 with a truce on November 29th.

When his wife died in January of 1402, and Gian Galeazzo died in September, the political equilibrium was upset. Teodoro remarried in 1403, to Margherita, the daughter of Amedeo d'Acaia.

Next in this line was Giangiacomo (1395-1445). Teodoro wanted him to be involved in state affairs from early in his life. In 1404, his name already appeared on a document alongside his father's. At fifteen, he was summoning military contingents and appointing officials. In 1406, it was proposed that he marry Giovanna, the younger sister of

Amedeo VIII of Savoy. The dowry was fixed at 60,000 florins. The wedding took place on January 4, 1411. From 1411 to 1413 he was his father's lieutenant and managed internal affairs of state.

When his father passed, he assumed full power and by 1418 his authority extended to the Principality of Piedmont. From 1425-1429, he fought several short wars. At least from March 1411, signed the documents as a hereditary prince. This was expressly confirmed to him on 26 March 1414 in Acqui with a diploma from the emperor Sigismund, who in that year stayed for about four months in the Monferrato area, as a guest of the Marquises of Monferrato.

In the following months he was engaged in military actions on the border with the Genoese territory against the Doge Tomasso Fregoso in agreement with the Duke of Milan Filippo Maria Visconti. On the strength of recent conquests, he reconfirmed its authority over the Del Carretto marquises and other small lords in the Apennine area.

Also, in 1425, against the policy of equilibrium among Italian states, the story began, with the intentions of Amedeo VIII, to lead to the complete absorption of the Marquisate of Monferrato by the Dukes of Milan and Savoy. In December, Florence and Venice joined forces to oppose the expansionism of Filippo Maria Visconti, also soliciting the agreement of Amedeo VIII and Giangiacomo joined on 11 July 1426 and in the short war that followed against the Visconti bought land between Biella and Vercelli.

After a brief resumption of the war, on 2 December 1427, Giangiacomo agreed with the Duke of Milan giving him his daughter Maria in marriage. Giangiacomo who had continued to have relations with Milan and Venice at the same time without knowing, which side to take, and became suspicious of both interlocutors, and only on 13 April, 1428 ended up making an agreement with the Venetians on the promise of aid and the dispatch of a commissioner to Monferrato.

Relations with Milan worsened further in 1430. In February 1431, with the resumption of the war between Venice and the Visconti, hostilities also opened in Monferrato with mutual raids. With the Venetian assent in spring Giangiacomo occupied the lands of the lords of Cocconato, the Turco and the bishop of Asti, allies of the Visconti, but the Monferrato forces to the left of the Po disbanded in front of their adversaries. At the same time Amedeo VIII and the Duke of Milan entered into a secret pact which aimed at dividing the Marquisate to the detriment of Montefeltro. In 1433, by signing the new peace of Ferrara, Visconti was forced to accept the restitution of the Monferrato territories he occupied.

Giangicomo was not, at first sight, as inept and cowardly as his political and military misadventures might lead us to believe. He had the misfortune of having to compete with masters of intrigue such as Amedeo VIII of Savoy and Filippo Maria Visconti and, in the military field, with the greatest leaders of the time: Niccolò Piccinino and Francesco Sforza. The chronicler, Galeotto Del Carretto defines him as "pleasant, pious, benign, cheerful, joyful and full of virtue" this brief and commendable profile contrasts in part with some traits of his attitudes and tastes that emerge from the Savoy, Milan and Venetian correspondence. [4]

Bonifacio III (1426-1494) assumed power when his brother William VIII died in 1483, leaving no male heir. He was married three times and I descend from his third marriage to Maria of Serbia the daughter of the Serbian Stefan Brankovic.[5] His son William IX (1486-1518) assumed power when he was only eight years old. At first his mother was regent, and later his mother's cousin assumed that role. He continued the pro-French policies of his father and in 1508 he married Princess Anna d'Alencon.

In 1513, he covered the French retreat form Milan, but was forced to pay Maximillian Sforza 30,000 scudi to avoid retaliation. Sforza did not respect the agreement and his troops invaded Montferrat.[6] His daughter, Margherita, married Federico Gonzaga and two of their sons were the Dukes of Mantua.[7]

William IX by Macrino d'Alba (born c.1460–
65; died c.1510–20), Public domain, via Wikimedia Commons

Margherita by Giulio Romano, Public domain, via
Wikimedia Commons

[143]

Orsini

Orsini is an important Roman family whose story is documented with certainty from the end of the tenth century. I have at least 63 ancestors from this old and noble family. There are 5 Popes (Stephen II, 752-757; Paul I, 757-767; Celestine III, 1191-1198; Nicholas III, 1277–1280; and Benedict XIII, 1724-1730 and 34 Cardinals from this family.[1]

The power of the Orsini was affirmed. With Orso Di Bobone (12th century), a relative of Pope Celestine III, who was his protector. While this family goes back to the 10th century AD, the earliest person I can confidently trace back to is my 28th great-grandfather Pietro (1070-1159), who may or may not have been Chancellor of Rome. The first in this line of any real notoriety is Giovanni (1155-1232), also known as, "Giangaetano." He was a Roman Nobleman and Lord of Vicovaro, Licentiate, Roccagiovine, Bardella, Ampollione, Cantalupo, Porcile, and Nettuno from 1191. In 1215, he bought the Castle of Civitella. He married Stefania Rossi and his cousin was Pope Celestino III.

His son, my 24th great-grandfather Matteo, also known as "il Grande" was a Senator of Rome (1178-1246). He valiantly opposed the rivals of his family and defended the city from Frederick II. His first wife Perna was my great-grandmother. His son Gentile was the father of Bertoldo (1221-1318), my 23rd great- grandfather and Elisabetta, my 22nd great-grandmother, who married Gofreddo Caetani.

Gentile II (1255-1314) was my 21st great-grandfather. He was Senator of Rome in 1280, 1286, 1287, 1300, 1304, and 1306. In 1301, Mayor of Orvieto and also the Grand Justice of the Kingdom of Naples in 1297. And the Captain Justice Abruzzo in 1296. He married three times, and his second marriage was to my great-grandmother Clarice Ruffo from the Counts of Catanzaro.

Gentile's son Romano (1268-1327) was the First Count of Nola and Soana in 1292. He was Grand Executioner of Naples and Royal

Vicar of Rome in 1326. He married Anastasia Montfort in 1293. Romano's son Roberto (1295-1345) was also the Grand Executioner of Naples and my 21st great-grandfather. In addition to holding many of Romano's titles, he was also Chamberlain of the King of Naples and Counselor of Basilicata. Roberto married Sveva Del Balzo, daughter of Ugo, the Count of Spoleto.

Roberto's son Nicola (1331-1399) was also the Grand Executioner of Naples. Seems as if everyone was trained for this or no one else wanted the job. Once again, he held most of the titles of his father and grandfather, with the addition of Senator of Rome in 1356, Viceroy of Abruzzo in 1359, Gonfoloniere of Santa Roma Church in 1363, Vicar of Orvieto in 1367, Governor of Heritage in 1371, and Grand Chancellor of the Kingdom of Naples from 1383. He married Giovanna de Sabran, the daughter of Guglielmo, Count of Ariano. Nicola's first son Robert (1360-1400) was the Fourth Earl of Nola, and he was in the service of Joan I, Queen of Naples. Robert's illegitimate son Pirro (d 1420) was the Fifth Earl of Nola and the Grand Executioner.

Nicola's second son, and my 19th great-grandfather, was Raimondo, aka "Raimondello" Orsini del Balzo (1361-1406). Raimondo was Count of Soleto and Lord of Benevento and Flumeri, appointed by Pope Urban IX. He was later the First Prince of Taranto and Lord of about a dozen other fiefdoms. He later renounced Benevento and Flumeri in exchange for 75,000 Ducati ($11,250,000 roughly). Having lent the Pope 50,000 Ducati, he obtained the tithes from the Kingdoms of Sicily and Brindisi. He was the Duke of Bari, and Captain of the Land of Bari and Otranto in 1382. In 1384, he was Captain General of the Duke of Anjou. He was the Gonfaloniere of the Holy Roman Church and Protector of the Kingdom of Sicily in 1385. Raimondo was also the Captain General of Otranto in 1399 and Royal Chamberlain and Knight of the Order of the Ship from 1382. He was, at the time, the richest Italian feudal lord and his income exceeded the income of the King of Sicily. He married Maria d'Enghien, Countess of Lecce. His daughter Celia, my 18th great-grandmother, married Antonio Sanseverino, Duke of San Marco. Another daughter, Catherine was my 15th great-grandmother, and she married Tristano of Chiaramonte. [2]

Geronima Orsini

Another line down from Romano links me to my 13th great-grandmother, Geronima Orsini (1503-1570). Geronima married Pier Luigi I, the Duke of Parma, and the son of Pope Paul III. Her father was Ludivico (d 1534), the Eighth Count of Pitigliano, Lord of Soriano and many other fiefdoms, and Conservator of Orvieto.

Ludivico's father was Niccolo (1442-1510), the Sixth Earl of Pitigliano and Count of Nola. Several of his fiefs were confiscated by the King of Naples in 1495, with the accusation of treason. He was Marshall and Captain General of the Republic of Florence, and Governor of the Venitian Militias. He married Elena Conti. In 1471, he deposed his father Aldobrandino II (d 1472).

Gian Girdano by Unknow Person, Public domain, via Wikimedia Commons

The Fourth Earl of Pitigliano was Niccolo I (d 1425), who married Luigia Orsini. The Third Earl was Bertoldo (d 1417), also Lord of Sorano and about six other fiefdoms. He was also Vicar of Canino. The second Earl was Aldobrandino (d 1384), who married Mabilia, daughter of Palantine Count, Benedetto Caetani. Aldobrandino's father Guido (d 1348) was the First Earl of Pitigliano and Soana, and Lord of Manciano, Saturnia, and Sorano. In 1342, he was the Captain General of Perugia. He married Agostina, the daughter of Gherado I, Count of Donaritico.

I, Sailko, CC BY-SA 3.0 <https://crea-tivecommons.org/licenses/by-sa/3.0>, via Wikimedia Commons

Felice Orsini

My 12th great-grandmother from this family was Felice Orsini (d 1596), who married Marcantonio Colonna II, Prince and Duke of Paliano in 1552. Her father Girolamo (d 1545) was Lord of Bracciano, Campagnano, Galeria, and several other fiefdoms. He was also Prince to the Papal Throne.

Girolamo was the son of Gian Girdano (d 1517), the Ninth Earl of Tagliacozzo and Albe, as well as Lord of several other fiefdoms. He was Prince to the Papal Throne and Knight of the Order of St Michael. He married twice, first to Maria Cecilia d'Aragona and the second time to my great-grandmother Felice Della Rovere, the daughter of Pope Julius II. Another son of Gian's was Gentile Virgilio (1498-1548), Count of Anguiliara, who was General Admiral of the Papal fleet and French Admiral. His daughter, Caterina married Troiano Spinelli, Prince of Scalea.

Felice Orsini: Scipione Pulzone, Public domain, via Wikimedia Commons

Gian's father was Gentil Virginio (d 1497 by poison). Besides being the Eighth Earl of Tagliacozzo and Albe, he was Baron of Cerbara, and Lord of Bracciano, Campagnano, Galeria, and several other fiefdoms. In addition, he was Count of dell'Anguillara, Lord of Monterano, Cerveteri and other fiefdoms. He was also Knight of the Ermine from 1463 and Grand Constable of the Kingdom of Naples. His fiefdoms were confiscated in 1495 for felony of treason. He was married to Isabella Orsini, daughter of Raimondo, the First Prince of Salerno.

Next in this line was my 16th great-grandfather Napoleone (d 1480). As Lord of Bracciano, he built Odescalchi Castle. He was the Seventh Earl of Tagliacozzo and Albe, and he was also Baron of Cerbara. He was a leader in the Kingdom of Naples and owned forty-three fiefdoms in the Kingdom of Naples. He married Francesca Orsini. His father Carlo (d 1445) was Lord of Bracciano, Pacentro, Lamentana, Trevignano, Scrofano, Bardella, and Fornello. He was also Grand Constable of the Kingdom of Sicily under Queen Giovanna II. He married Paola Geronima Orsini from the Counts of Tagliacozzo. His father, Giovanni (d 1393) was Lord of Nerola and several other fiefdoms. He was married to Bartolomea Spinelli, daughter of Nicola, Count of Gioia and Grand

Chancellor of the Kingdom of Sicily. Giovanni's, grandfather, and my 20th great-grandfather was Giacomo (d 1306), who was appointed by King Charles II of Sicily as the Second Earl of Tagliacozzo and Lord of several fiefdoms. In 1271 and 1273, he was War Captain of Todi, and in 1278, the Podesta of Todi. He married Matteuccia Orsini. Giacomo's father Napoleone II (d 1282) was the first Earl of Tagliacozzo, invested by the Pope in 1253. [3]

Caterina Orsini

Caterina is another 16th great-grandmother (1420-1504) and comes from the Dukes of Gravina and Princes of Solofra, which began with her father Francesco Orsini (d 1456). She was married to the Lord of Sermoneta. Francesco was the Royal Counselor and Marshall of the Kingdom of Sicily on behalf of King Ladislao I. Later, he was Captain General of Queen Giovanna II. In 1420, he was the Ambassador to Barcelona, and in 1443 and 1447, the Ambassador to Rome. He was the First Count and later Duke of Gravina, and Count of Campagna and Conversano. In 1421, he was the Lord of Monopoli and Count of Copertino. He served the kings of Naples, the pope, Florence, and Venice. He was married to Margherita Della Marra and was the brother of Carlo mentioned above. [4]

Pignatelli

The Pignatelli family is an ancient Neapolitan family that I can trace back to my 27th great-grandfather Lucio who was the Constable of Naples in 1102. It is thought that the family originated in Lombardy long before that date. Over the course of centuries, they were Lords of Caserta, held the seats of Nido and Portanova in Naples and were princes of several areas around Naples. [1]

I enter this line through my 8th great-grandmother Princess Geromina Pignatelli (1644-1711). She married Prince Francesco Caracciolo. It is through Geromina, that I am a direct descendant of Hernando Cortes.

I have many direct ancestors in this family here are some of the most recent and most prominent figures.

Geromina's father was Ettore (1620-1674). He inherited the Duchy of Monteleone, the County of Borello and the Baronies of Mesiano and Rosarno. From his mother, he also received the Grandate of Spain. After marrying Giovanna Tagliavia d'Aragona, the daughter of Diego, Prince of Castelventrano and Duke of Terranova, he was qualified as Marquis del Vaglio. Giovanna's mother descended from Hernando Cortes. They married in Palermo in 1639 with great fanfare.

He distinguished himself in the mid-century Spanish revolt and eventually was appointed president of the Province of Catanzaro by Don Giovanni of Austria. He continued to live in Sicily and part of the Council of State of Sicily. When his father-in-law passed away, he took over the offices of great Almirante and great Constable of Sicily. In 1666, as Grand Chamberlain of the Kingdom of Naples. Ferdinand III granted the Dukes and Duchesses of Terranova the title of Prince of the Holy Roman Empire with rights of transmission to all descendants in 1648.

In 1667-68, Ettore became a Viceroy of Aragon, a position his father Fabrizio held before him. And in 1670, he became a Knight of the Golden Fleece.[2]

Another link into this line is through my 5th great-grandmother Maria Giuseppa Pignatelli. Her father was Ferdinando I (1689-1767). He was the Prince of Strongoli, Duke of Tolve and Count of Melissa. He fought in Spain for Charles III, then in Hungary against the Turks, and later in Sicily in the Fourth Alliance War. In 1727, he was General Field Officer and in 1733 General Field Marshal. In 1734, Charles VI made him Grand Admiral of the Kingdom of Sicily. In 1739, he was made a Knight of the Golden Fleece. Finally, in 1740, he was promoted to General of Field Majors. [3] His father was Niccolo (1648-1730) the Viceroy of Sardinia, and his mother was Giovanna Pignatelli.

Niccolo's father was Giulio Pignatelli (1587-1658) the second Prince of Noia. His father was Fabrizio (1568-1627) Prince of Noia and Marquis of Cerchiaro who was married to Giovanna Spinelli.

My 11th great-grandfather in this line was Fabrizio (d 1567) He was a general in the service of Spain and freed Calabria from Turkish raids. He was also General Field Master in the Flanders wars and fought in Tripoli. He founded the Pellegrini hospital in Naples. [4]

Unknown author, Public domain, via
Wikimedia Commons

Ruffo

The Ruffo family goes back to the Emperors of Constantinople. They were a rich and powerful family with vast holdings in Calabria and Sicily. Many in the family were Grandees of Spain and awarded various knightly orders, such as, The Golden Fleece, San Gennaro, and the Grand Cross of St. Ferdinand. It is one of the Serene Seven Houses of the Kingdom of Sicily.[xi] I have fifty ancestors in this line.

I can trace back to Gervasio Ruffo, my 22nd great-grandfather who was made Lord of Mizzillicar by Roger II of Sicily. His son Pietro is the founder of the family.

Giovanni my 19th great-grandfather was Lord of Policastro, Lubianco, Misuraca, Simari, Torre della Marina and Rocca Bernarda. In addition, he was Captain General of Calabria and Chancellor of the Kingdom of Sicily in 1239. Eventually he went into exile in Rome and returned to Sicily in 1266.

Giovanni's son Fulcone was made an Armed Knight by Emperor Frederick II in 1247. He was Lord of Santa Cristina and Placanica. He was the second Lord of Sinopoli, Seminara and Bovalino.

Fulcone's son Enrico (d 1309) was the third Lord of Sinopoli, Lord of Seninaram Santa Cristina and several other fiefdoms. He was also Chamberlain of the King of Naples and Viceroy of Terra di Lavoro. In 1278, he was made and armed knight by King Charles I and in 1283 he received the title of Nobleman by royal decree.

Next in line is my 16th great-grandfather Guglielmo (d 1361) in addition to inheriting Enrico's titles, he was Lord of Pietracicara and Artesicolo. He was Viceroy and Grand Justice of the Principality Ultra in 1323 and first Earl of Sinopoli in 1334. In 1335 he was Captain General of the Abruzzi and Viceroy of Calabria. His second wife Eloisa d'Erville was my 16th great-grandmother and brought a dowry of one hundred ounces of gold. Another son of Enrico's was my 15th great-grandfather Fulcone (1334-1391). He was the second Earl of Sinopoli, he was married four times and I descend from his first wife Maria Sambiase.

Fulcone's son Guglielmo (d 1415) was my 14th great-grandfather and third Earl of Sinopoli. He was a royal councilor. He married Lucrezia Caracciolo who brought a dowry of 900 gold ounces. Their son Carlo (1390-1464) was the fourth Earl of Sinopoli, Lord of Bagnara, Motta Rossa, Belcore, Massanova and several other fiefdoms, including Sciacca. He was Councilor to the King of Naples and Viceroy of Calabria in 1445. His first wife and my great-grandmother was Guglielma Caterina Grimaldi who brought a dowry of 3600 Ducati. Another son Nicola Antonio started the Ruffo Di Bagnara and Castelcicala branch of the family.[xii]

Nicola Antonio was the Lord of Vecchio Bruzzano and married Elisabetta Ruffo the daughter of Enrico the Count of Condolanni. His son Esau (d 1510) was a 15th great-grandfather Lord of Bagnara, Bruzzano and Condolanni and Grand Chancellor of the Kingdom of Naples. Esau's son Bernardo (d 1515) was Lord of Bagnara and married Isabella Mastroguidice. Two of their children are my great-grandparents. Guglielmo my 13th great-grandfather (d 1539) was Lord of Bagnara and Solano and married Antonia Spadafora and Diana, my 13th great-grandmother who married Giovanni Claver Baron of Casoleto.

Bernardo's son Giovanni Giacomo (d 1582) was Lord of Bagnaro and Solano and married Ippolita Spinelli, daughter of Salvatore the Marquis Fuscaldo. Their son Carlo (1566-1610), my 10th great-grandfather, was the first Duke of Bagnara as well as Lord of Sant'Antimo, Solano and Fiumara. He married Antonia Spadafora, daughter of Federico Barone del Biscotto.

Francesco (1596-1643) was my 9th great-grandfather and the second Duke of Bagnara, as well as lord of the same fiefdoms held by his father. He married Guiomara Ruffo, daughter of Vincenzo of the princes of Scilla. Their son Paolo (1617-1671) was known as Duke of Tufara and he married Vittoria Pignatelli, daughter of Ludovico Marquis of Casalnuovo. My 7th great-grandfather Fabrizio Ruffo (1648-1720) was the first Baron of Castelcicala and married Guiomara Ruffo.

My 8th great-grandfather Vincenzo (1622-1680) did not hold any titles and his son Francesco was called the Duke of Melito as his wife Teodora Alberti was Duchess of Melito and Marchesa of Pentidatillo. At this point it gets a little fuzzy, but a Donna Maria Imara Francone married Luigi Caracciolo the second Prince of Torchiarolo, where I enter this family. I say it gets fuzzy because there are records of an Imara Ruffo marrying her cousin Paolo Ruffo and a Paolo Francone.

Going back to Fulcone his son Pietro II (1231-1302) held many of the same titles as his father, plus the second Earl of Catanzaro. He also was the Horseman Major of King Charles I of Anjou, Lord of Briatico and Calvello. In 1283 he added Cotone and in 1290 he claimed over another dozen fiefdoms. In 1292 he added Carbonara. He was assassinated in 1302 in Catanzaro. He married Giovanna d'Aquino, daughter of Thomas II third Earl of Acerra. Their daughter Claricia married Gentle Orsini.[xiii]

Saluzzo

The Saluzzo were the medieval rulers of Saluzzo in Piedmont and the bordering fiefdoms from 1175 to 1549. At one time, they were earls, but were given marquis rank by the Emperor Frederick I. In 1549, during the Italian Wars, Saluzzo was annexed to France and in 1601, it was ceded to the Duke of Savoy. The first Marquis of Saluzzo was my 24th great-grandfather Manfredo I (1130-1175) his father was Bonifacio del Vasto Margrave of Liguria.[1] Manfredo's son, Manfredo II (1157-1215) was known as "Punasio" (stinking nose) due to a physical defect.[2]

Bonifacio (1180-1212) was married to Maria of Torres and as he died before his father the title passed to his son Manfredo III (1204-1244) [3] Next in line was Tomasso (1234-1296) he married Beatrice of Savoy, the daughter of count Amedeo IV. This marriage began the Marquise's surrender to Savoy. [4]

Under the leadership of my 20th-great-grandfather Tomasso I (1234-1296) Saluzzo blossomed achieving greatness. Tomasso created borders that lasted for over

Unknown author, Public domain, via Wikimedia Commons

two centuries. He was often at odds with Asti and was a prime enemy of Charles of Anjou. During his reign, he made Saluzzo a free city and created a podesta to rule in his name. He married Luisa of Ceva.[5]

His son Manfredo IV (d 1330) continued the extension of the Margraviate by obtaining the castles of Cairo Montenotte, Rochetta and Cortemilia. His first wife, from whom I descend was Beatrice of Sicily, who was, the daughter of Manfredo of Sicily. They had one son, Federico (1287-1336), who by rights was heir. However, Manfredo tried to appoint his second son as heir, urged by his second wife. This event precipitated a civil war between the half-brothers for two years, in which Federico took the throne.[6] He was only margrave for four years.

Federico was succeeded by his son Tomasso II (1304-1357). To-masso's mother was Margarete de La Tour du Pin, who was the daughter of Humbert I the Dauphin de Viennois. His uncle, Manfredo disputed his succession, and this issue caused another war within the family. With the support of Robert King of Naples, Manfredo won and sacked the city of Saluzzo and set it on fire. He also imprisoned his nephew and forced him to pay a ransom. In 1347, Tomasso joined the marquis of Montferrat and Humber II of Viennois in attacking the Savoy and conquering Angevin lands in the north of Italy.[7]

Unknown author, Public domain, via Wikimedia Commons

The next marquis was Federico II (1396), who inherited a marquise ravaged by civil war. Consequently, he petitioned help from France and in 1375, he swore allegiance to Charles, the Dauphine of France.

His son and my 16th great-grandfather in this line was Tomasso III (1380-1415). My 16th great-grandfather's mother was Beatrice of Geneva. Because of his father's allegiance to the French throne, he spent most of his younger years in Provence. In 1394, he was captured by the Savoy and imprisoned first in Savigliano and then in Turin. He was freed after two years after paying 20,000 gold florins. He was married to Marguerite of Pierrepont and they had five children, two of which are in my line. Giovanna who married Guy Lord of Maillet and Offermont and Ricciardia who married Niccolo III d'Este.[8]

Unknown author, Public domain, via Wikimedia Commons

I believe that my 3rd great-grandmother Maria Costanza Saluzzo (1781-1858) traces back to the ancient line, but I cannot confirm with certainty to whom. I do know that her father Duke Agostino (1743-1783) was ascribed to the Seat of the Nile in Naples and that all his descendants were entitled to the title of prince and count of the Austrian Empire. Agostino's father was Giacomo (b 1709) and married Giuseppa Pignatelli.

I also know that they moved to Genoa and then in 1606, the family moved to Naples when Agostino bought Sanseverino. [9]

Unknown author, Public domain, via Wikimedia Commons

Unknown author, Public domain, via Wikimedia Commons

Sambiase

The Sambiase family is a branch of the Sanseverino family which took the name from a fiefdom in Calabria. They were nobles of Cosenza, Lecce, and Naples, and were assigned to the throne of Portanova. It is thought that they most likely descend from Rollo the Duke of Normandy. [1]

The earliest in this line is my 23rd great-grandfather Rainone. Giacomo, my 21st great-grandfather was the first Lord of Sambiase and Lacconia. His grandson Riccardo, the third Lord of Sambiase and Lacconia sold the fiefdom of Lacconia in 1260.

Ruggero II, the fourth Lord of Sambiase and my 18th great-grandfather was the War Captain of Cosenza. He had an annuity of 40 ounces of gold and was the Counselor to Robert I, King of Sicily. In 1310, he was the Viceroy of Calabria and in 1316 bought the fiefdom of Pietrapaolo from the Count of Gravina. He later inherited Luzzi and Noce upon the death of his first wife Maria Squilla.

My 17th great-grandfather was Filippo, Lord of Sant'Antonio who upon the death of his brother Matteo, became the Lord of Rochetta and Porcile. He was married twice to my Great Grandmother Violante, the daughter of Filippo Tordi, Field Master of the Neapolitan Army and then Chiara Martorano of the Lords of Tortora.

Filippo's great-grandson, Giovannello, was the Patrizio of Cosenza, Lord of Scala and Pioetrapaolo, his first wife, Bererdesca Migliarino was the daughter of Niccolo, the Captain of the City of Naples. His son Giovanni Andrea started the Cosenza branch.

My 7th great-grandmother Ippolita (b 1670) from this family married Prince Giacomo Capece Zurlo. Her mother was Victoria Mandatoricci the third Duchess of Crosia. [2]

Sanseverino

The Sanseverino family were feudal lords since the time of Charles I Anjou. They were nobility in the Seat of Porto in Naples. It was originally thought that the family originated in Siena and came to Naples, but some believe that it came from Casale di Fratta. The accepted progenitor of the family is my 34th great-grandfather Ruggero (d 1082) a Norman Knight, possibly the son of Crispino Lord of Arnes and from the lineage of the Duke of Normandy Rollo. His grandson also named Ruggero (d 1125) was the Lord go Sanseverino and Rota and Lord of all the castles of the Rota valley. After the death of his wife Sica from the Dukes of Gaeta, he become a monk and donated most of his lands and vassals. [1]

My entry into this family is with my 15th great-grandmother, Gozzolina (b 1468) who married Diomede Carafa the fourth Earl of Maddaloni. Her father Girolamo (1448-1487) was possibly executed by the order of King Ferdinand I of Naples. He was the second Prince of Bisignano, fourth duke of San Marco, seventh Earl of Tricarico, seventh Earl of Chiaromonte and count of several other lands. He was the Grand Camerario of the Kingdom of Naples but implicated in the conspiracy of the barons and arrested with his children sent into exile. He married Giovannella in 1465 with a dowry of 12,000 Ducati. She was the daughter of Baldassarre Count of Morcone and Antonella Caracciolo.

Diomede's father was Luca (1420-1470) He bought Bisignano for 20,000 Ducati and San Chirico, Lauria and Saponara for 8,000 Ducati, he owned the lands mentioned above under his son. He married Gozzollina Ruffo.

Luca's father Antonio (1396-1430) was the second duke of San Marco, fifth Earl of Tricarico and fifth Earl of Chiaromonte. He founded the convent of San Domencio di Cosenza. He married Giovannella Del Balzo the natural daughter of Raimondo Prince of Taranto. His father Ruggero (1376-1430) was fourth Earl of Tricarico and fourth Earl of Chiaromonte.

Vincenzo (b 1355) my 20th great-grandfather was executed with his cousins by order of King Ladislao of Naples for treason. He was the third Count of Tricarico and third Count of Chiaramonte. He was also the first Duke of Venosa that he later renounced to become the first Duke of Amalfi. He married Margarita di Sangineto the Countess of Altamonte. His father Ruggero (1312-1362) was Earl of Chiaramonte and Tricarico and Captain General of Calabria in 1348.

The first Earl of Tricarico and Chiaromonte was Giacomo my 21st great-grandfather who started the Princes of Bisignano line (1290-1348). He was also Lord of Castronova, Noia, Torremare and Seviso. He married Margherita Chiaromonte daughter of Riccardo the Count of Chiaromonte. His older brother Enrico was my 23rd great-grandfather (d 1314) was the fourth Earl of Marisco, Lord of Curraco, Grand Constable of Naples. He married Ilaria De Lloria Baroness of Lauria. Their father was Tomasso (1252-1324) Earl of Marisco, Baron of Sanseverino, Lord of Centola, Polla and Curraco from 1291. He was also Lord of Posiglione, Lord of Sanza and several other fiefdoms from 1294 through 1301 and in 1305 Lord of Policastro. He married three times. His second wife Margaret of Vaudemont the daughter of the Count of Vaudmont was Enrico's mother and his third wife Sveva d'Avezzano was Giacomo's mother.

Tomasso's father was Ruggero (1237-1285) Earl of Marisco confirmed by King Manfredi I of Sicily. He was also Baron of Sanseverino, Lord of Dian, Sala and Athena invested by Charles I Anjou. As the Captain General of the king of Sicily in 1285, he took part in the battle of Benevento. His second wife, Theodora d'Aquino was Tomasso's mother.

Ruggero's father was also Tomasso (d 1246) who died as part of a revolt against the Emperor Frederick II. The leaders were put in the stronghold of Cappaccio and left without water. They were executed by being hanged, quartered, burned alive or placed in bags and thrown into the sea. He was Earl of Marisco and Lord of Sanseverino. [2]

Sforza

This Noble family was started by my 19th Great Grandfather Muzio Attandolo who was a rich landowner of Cotignola in the mid-14th century.

My 17th great-grandfather was Muzio Attandolo Sfroza (1369-1424). He was at one time Captain of the Pope's People and served Boldrino de Panicale, Guido d'Asciano, Alberico da Barbiano and Cercolo Broglia. He later served as Viscount to the Kings of Naples. He was Count of Cotignola, and in 1412 Grand Constable of the Kingdom of Naples with an income of 8,000 Ducati. What's more, he was Lord of more than half a dozen fiefdoms. He married three times and had at least fifteen children, most of whom appear to have been illegitimate. He drowned in the Pescara River. During his life, he was in the service of Giovanna II the Queen of Naples, and later Pope Martin V whom Giovanna sent him to help in 1419. After falling out with Giovanna II, he sided with Louis III of Anjou. Eventually, he reconciled with Giovanna who had adopted his son Alfonso V. He was an excellent soldier and through his marriages knew how to increase and consolidate his wealth.[1]

Muzio Sforza

Petri Krohn, Public domain, via Wikimedia Commons

His son Alessandro, baptized Gregory, changed his name to Alessandro in honor of Pope Alexander V (1409-1473). He was a leader in the service of the Church and the King of Naples. He was also Vicar of the Church in Ancona in 1434 and Assisi in 1439. Duke of Sora, but not for very long. In 1463, he became lord of Gradara and Castelnuovo. In the same year, he was also the Grand Constable of Naples. His daughter Batista, from his first wife, Costanza Varano, married Federico III Montefeltro the Duke of Urbino.[2]

Although not in my direct line, one note of interest is that Alessandro's grandson Giovanni I (1466-1510) married the infamous Lucrezia Borgia, the daughter of Pope Alexander VI in 1493. The marriage annulled in 1497. Lucrezia also had an affair for many years with my 13th great-grandfather, Francesco Gonzaga.

Alessandro Sforza

National Gallery of Art, CC0, via Wikimedia Commons

Spinola

The Spinola family is from Genoa and one of the four largest noble houses. The first in the family to use the name Spinola was Guido (1102-1156). During the age of Fredrick II, they were the head of the Ghibelline party. For hundreds of years, they were a source of power in northern Italy. The family contributed three archbishops to Genoa and thirteen Cardinals.[1]

I enter the family with my 7th great-grandmother Antonia (1659-1744) who married Prince Marino Caracciolo III in 1688.

Antonia's father was Paolo Vincenzo (1632-1699) he was the Marquis of Los Balbases and Duke of Sesto. He was the son of Filippo Spinola and Geromina Doria. Paolo followed the military traditions of the family and served the Spanish Monarch. He participated in the against France beginning in 1649. In 1650 he commanded two companies of horses with valor. He took part in the sieges of Trino, Crescentino and Casale. Later, he participated in the liberation of Pavia, commanded troops sent to rescue Alexandria and then defeated the army of the Duke of Modena. After fighting in several battles from 1656 to 1659, he was appointed general of the calvary. He married Anna Colonna in 1653 who was the daughter of Marcantonio the prince of Paliano.

He held the office the governor of the state of Milan for two terms between 1668 and 1670 and then was appointed ambassador to the court of Vienna. In 1677 he was the ambassador to Paris, as part of his official role, he concluded the marriage of the daughter of the Duke of Orleans to the King of Spain. Four of his daughters were nuns in Milan, and his other daughters entered into marriages with high-ranking Spanish nobles.[2]

Paolo Vincenzo's father was Filippo (1594-1659) son of the commander general of the Spanish Army in Flanders. He lived in the court of King Philip III from 1607 and served as a page to Queen Margaret of Austria-Styria. After the Queen's death in 1611, he returned to Italy. Due to his father's standing with the Spanish court, he was provided with a pension of 400 scudi a month. He made his debut in the army of Flanders and he then was the general commander of the calvary in Milan. In 1630, with an army of 5,000 infantry and 500 calvary, he took Pontestura, San Giorgio Monferrato and Rosignano but was unable to prevent the French from entering Casale.

Filippo Spinola

Anthony van Dyck, Public domain, via Wikimedia Commons

In 1631, he was granted the honor of the Order of the Golden Fleece. In 1634 appointed general of the calvary in the state of Milan. He returned to the court of the King of Spain in Madrid in 1635 and was made the Commander Major of Castile. He returned to active service in 1639 when the French conquered Salses. Filippo encircled the French forcing them to surrender. He was recalled to the court of Philip IV in 1655. He was married to Geromina Doria.[3]

Paolo's father and my 10th great-grandfather, was Ambrogio (1569-1630). He had a passion for history, geography, and mathematics, but his brother chose a military career for him. In 1601 he planned, with his brother Federico, to arm a fleet capable of attacking England. In 1602 he enlisted 9,000 soldiers to attack Flanders. In 1605, he was appointed general field master, with the authority over all the armies of Flanders, he was also appointed with the title of Knight of the Order of the Golden Fleece. The war went on for several year until a truce was signed in April of 1609. He returned to active service in 1620 at the request of Emperor Ferdinand II. He remained in Brussels until 1628 and went to Spain and remained there until the second half of 1629. In July of that year, he was appointed governor of Milan. He was married to Giovannetta Bacciadonna.[4]

Anthony van Dyck, Public domain, via Wikimedia Commons

Spinelli

The Spinelli family is one of the oldest families in Naples and were feudal lords since the time of the Normans. They held some of the most illustrious orders of chivalry, including the Order of the Golden Fleece, Royal Order of San Gennaro, and the Grand Cross of San Fernando. They also held the Seat of the Nile in Naples.[1]

I can trace back confidently to my 16th great-grandfather Troiano prior to that, the line is not very clear. His son was Giacomo (d 1474). Giacomo's son was Troiano (d 1485). He was the first Baron of Summonte and participated in the Parliament of the Nobles in 1443 and was in the service of Alfonso V of Aragon. He married Maria Caracciolo, daughter of Gaultieri and Martuscella Piscicelli.

Troiano's son Carlo (d 1540) was the first Baron of Seminara, that he bought for 4,000 Ducati in 1495. He later obtained the fief of Santa Cristina in 1517 and was the first Count of Seminara in 1532. He is also the lord of Foscardo, Guardia Piedmont and Pantano. He married Eufemia Siscara the daughter of the Count of Aiello and Giulia Carafa.

Their son Paolo (d 1577) was Lord of Cosoleto, by succession from his wife, Cornelia the daughter of Jacopo Claver and Diana Ruffo of the Lords of Bagnara. Their daughter Victoria married Marizio Carafa, Duke of Madaloni. Their daughter, Roberta married Prince Camillo Caracciolo, which is where I enter this line.[2]

One other 17th great-grandmother in this line was Bartolomea Spinelli, whose father was Nicola the first Count of Gioia.

Visconti

The Visconti family originated in the tenth century as minor nobility. My 26th great-grandfather Eriprando (1050-1101) appears to be the first in the line, however I have found some farther back that I cannot confirm for certain. They gained real power in 1262 when Pope Urban IV appointed Ottone Visconti archbishop of Milan.[1]

MATTEO MAGNO VISCONTE

British Museum, Public domain, via Wikimedia Commons

My 21st great-grandfather was Matteo I (1250-1322). He was the son of Teobaldo and Anastasia Pirovano, also from a Milanese aristocracy. Teobaldo was beheaded in the square of Gallarte after being captured during a military action against the Della Torre. Matteo went into exile around the same time and married Bonacossa Burri. In 1277, the Della Torre forces were defeated, and the Visconti returned to Milan.

In 1287, he obtained the title of Captain of the People, a five-year office. Between 1290 and 1294, he became Captain of the People in Novara and Vercelli, conquered Como and became Captain of the people for the Marquisate of Monferrato. In 1302, Pope Boniface VIII supported an alliance against him, headed by the Della Torre who regained control of Milan. Matteo attempted to retake Milan several times in 1302, 1303 and 1306.

In 1310, the elected emperor Henry VII of Luxembourg allowed Matteo to return to Milan and proclaimed peace between the Visconti and Della Torre. In 1311, he had himself nominated as the imperial vicar of Milan, with a donation of 50,000 florins, for an indefinite period, until the money was returned. It never was, so he remained in power until 1317, when Pope John XXII revoked it. In 1318, the pope excommunicated Matteo and most of his allies. [2]

Two of Matteo's sons were great-grandfathers of mine. Stefano (1287-1327) is a 20th great-grandfather and Galeazzo (1277-1328) is a 19th great-grandfather. Stefano died after a banquet he gave to celebrate the crowning of Louis of Bavaria as King of Italy.[3] Galeazzo married Beatrice d'Este and spent his time at that court while in exile. In 1322, he was named Captain of the people in Milan. But because his cousin Lodrisio incited the uprising, he had to flee the city soon after. In 1328,

Michelino da Besozzo. Public domain. via Wikimedia Commons

with the help of Emperor Louis IV, he defeated an army sent by the pope. [4]

Galeazzo's daughter Ricciarda (1310-1366). Married Marquis Tomasso di Saluzzo. Stefano's son Barnarbo (1323-1385) married Beatrice Della Scala, together they had seventeen children. This marriage forged a bond between Milan and Verona. His ambitions kept him at war with Florence, Venice, Savoy, and Pope Urban V for many years. In 1350, he inherited the lands of Bergamo, Brescia, Cremona and Crema. In 1356, he was imprisoned by Markward von Randeck. In 1360, Pope Innocent declared him a heritic and he was condemned by Emperor Charles IV. In 1362, he attacked Mantua, and made peace with the pope, Urban V, but failed to return the Bologna and was excommunicated once again in 1363. Finally, in 1364, he left the Papal States and paid 500,000 Florins to end his contract. Bernarbo's twelfth child, Maddelena is my 18th great-grandmother who married Frederick the Duke of Bavaria.[5]

Galeazzo Visconti

Public Domain, https://commons.wiki-media.org/w/index.php?curid=30487

The Journey Home

After many months, thirty to be exact, we finally made our "Grand Rooting Trip" to Italy. Our plan was ambitious to say the least as we scheduled stops in five regions: Lazio, Molise, Campania, Calabria, and Sicily in fourteen days.

We made the stop in Rome, mainly so that the kids could see it and we had never made it to the Sistine Chapel. We also went to visit the tomb of Paul III, but unfortunately, we were not allowed to get to close.

The real "Rooting" part of the trip began once we arrived in Naples. We stayed in the historic district to be close to the action and were just off one of the narrow streets in the heart of the district, just a short walk to the Naples Archives and the Cathedral of Saint Maria Assunta, but also known as the Cathedral of San Gennaro.

To start the day, we did a walking tour with our guide Vincenzo that told us the history of Naples and about the Spaccanapoli, that was the street that divided old Naples in half. We then went to the first of the ancient homes of my Caracciolo ancestors the Hotel Caracciolo. Much larger in person than in the photos and we were able to go inside and see some of the common areas. Most of the stone floors, walls and columns are still in place and you can just imagine the parties that were held in the open courtyard. Across Via Carbonara there are the apartments where the Caracciolo family lived and where my great-grandmother Emilia was born and passed away. Not too far away is Vico Longo where the Sorrentino's resided, but apparently the area is not very good now and we were advised not to visit.

Arriving at the Duomo, we were met by Don Agostino Caracciolo di Torchiarolo, a distant cousin of my great-grandmother. Don Agostino was very gracious and gave us a tour of the San Gennaro part of the cathedral pointing out various statues and chapels and even the statue of a very distant cousin San Francesco Caracciolo. He also gave

us a book about the Caracciolo family throughout the ages. One thing to note, that I did not know was that the cathedral has markings on the floor that denote the break between the part that is owned by Rome and the part that is owned by Naples. In a deal centuries ago, it was agreed that the San Gennaro part of the church would be owned and cared for by Naples.

San Gennaro

Our next stop was the State Archives of Naples where we were met by the director Candida Carrino. She gave us a personal tour and showed us how parts of the old Benedictine Monastery were either under repair or in need of repair. In the center courtyard is a tree planted by St. Benedict hundreds of years ago, and when you stand there, you cannot hear the sounds of a bustling Naples outside. A very serene place in that heart of a large city. We saw one room that was filled with census books, and it was explained that when they removed some furniture, they found priceless frescos on the wall. Finally, we were let into a room that had the names of some of the most noble families of Naples, with their priceless collections. One of the historians created a Caracciolo display for us that included original handwritten family trees, crests and one document from a direct ancestor that was over one thousand years old.

Something that I learned on the trip that I did not know before was that the Piromallo family, besides having land in Calabria owned a lot of land in Cercola and Massa di Somma. We went for a family luncheon in Villa Egea in Massa di Somma and I met my cousin Cinzia Piromallo for the first time. We have been communicating on Facebook and in emails for years, but it was great to meet in person. I also got to meet my dad's first cousin Nicola Di Paolo that up until a few months before the trip, I never knew existed. A few days later, we had a real reunion in Torre Del Greco. After lunch, we went to the roof of the villa, and I was told that much of the land down that valley was Piromallo land.

One of the oldest Caracciolo records in the State Archives of Naples

Before we left Massa di Somma, we went to a small palazzo which I was told I had to see. Above the archway was the name of my third great-grandfather Cte. Giacomo Piromallo. As we walked through the arch and looked up, you could see the stemma of the family. Once through the arch, we were in a large courtyard, now a parking lot, but I would assume a garden or piazza back in the day. I was told to look up at the second floor window in the middle of the building. I was told that the Count would hold a party every year on his birthday and roast a pig. Wine would flow freely and then he would toss coins out of the window to watch the people fight over the money. Not a very pleasant story, but they seemed quite certain that this was a fact.

The next day, we got an early start and headed off to Capracotta the home of Count Giacomo's wife Beatrice Capece Piscicelli. It's a bit fuzzy to me as to when the Stemma and family names were merged, but it does seem that the family would visit various places owned by the Piromallo and Capece Piscicelli throughout the year. On our way there, we stopped at the Samnite archeological site outside of Pietrabbondante. The Samnites are considered to be the first "Italics" or Italians dating back to about 800 BC. Represented by the bull they fought and beat the Romans several times until finally losing and being absorbed

Home of Count Giacomo Piromallo near Naples

into the Roman Empire. The ruins consist of two temples, and amphitheater and several outbuildings. I have to say that the stone seats in the amphitheater were amazingly comfortable as the contoured to you back and you could not tell that you were sitting on stone. Author Nicola Mastronardi, an expert on the Samnite culture and the author of two books, met us there and gave us a brief history of the race. After that, we made a quick stop in to meet the mayor who gave us a plaque that celebrates the one-year anniversary of the Samnite Warrior statue in the piazza.

Arriving in Capracotta, we went to the town hall, which was the former home of the Dukes of Capracotta, and we were welcomed by the mayor, representatives of the town and several associations. After several speeches, the mayor presented us with several gifts and told us how grateful the people of the town were to know that US citizens wanted to visit. We then walked up to the church where Mass was ending. After mass, the priest announced to the congregation who we were and welcomed us as a family. To my surprise, no one left the church. Instead, they waited for my remarks and once again, we received a resounding welcome. The priest led us over to a side alter where three vestments were on display. These vestments, commissioned by my ancestors and made in Naples and are over 150 years old. You can plainly see the Stemma on the back. Inside the sacristy was a painting of the Madonna, one of five commissioned by the Capece Piscicelli that hangs in different churches around Italy.

Ancestral home of Duchess Beatrice Capece Piscicelli

Luncheon! Chef Michelle owner of L'Elfo created a special meal for us that was based on the food that the shepherds would eat as they moved the flock from Molise to Puglia. We were told that the duke had six-thousand sheep. The decor of L'Elfo takes you back in time with the wood and stone walls. Let me tell you, the meal was amazing. The starter was mashed potatoes with lentils, second was pasta with truffles, followed by a sheep stew. And of course, a great wine.

By now, we are pretty tired, but we still had to do an interview for Molise TV before going to the dress museum. The museum was created by Sebastiano Di Rienzo who was a designer for Valentino most of his career. Many of his creations are on display, we even got to try on some.

Our next stop was to see the snowplow that was gifted to the people of Capracotta by US citizens in 1950 and his still in use. Doctor Aldo Trotta read us his story about the delivery of the plow when he was seven years old. The plow has helped the town through several serious snowstorms for seventy years.

On the way out, we visited the statue that celebrates the Capracotese that emigrated to countries around the world.

The following day, we set out for Avellino, the seat of power for the Princes of Avellino for about two hundred years. I had no idea what to expect and then we arrived in the piazza, we saw the palace built by my 7th great-grandparents Prince Marino III and Donna Antonia Spinola from the Dukes of San Severino decked out in Italian flags. As we entered the courtyard, we were met by dignitaries from the region, people dressed in period costumes, and a trumpeter that announced our arrival. So, I stand there like a fool trying to figure out my next move.

Everyone was very nice and before going up into the palazzo we were asked to visit the new multimedia display set up to show the region. As you enter the room you, it appears as if you are flying through the region and you can see the hills, valleys castles and other prominent edifices. We were told that the Caracciolo princes brought industry and agriculture and to this day they are still very much appreciated by the people. After several speeches, exchange of gifts and of course excellent pastries we were led outside to tour other parts of the town.

As we walked to the duomo, several old buildings were pointed out, including the building where taxes were collected which is in the process of being refurbished. This building once had the statues of Prince Camillo and his son Prince Marino II on the roof. The Duomo is dedicated to Santa Maria Assunta was originally built in the 1100's. It is a very impressive church, and we were told the history and then were given a private tour. As we approached the altar, we saw three chairs. These chairs were used by the princes and their families and as I descend from them, we were allowed to actually take a seat. I have to admit, I did feel a sense of power. Below the church was the crypt for the monks. It was amazing to see how pristine this crypt was considering it was refurbished in the 1600's. As we left the church, we were met by Giovanni Spiniello a local artist whose studio is just off to the side of the church. We received a quick tour and he explained how his art is based on the earth and nature.

As we walked towards the hunting lodge and garden of the princes, we passed by the ruins of the original palazzo. While there is not much left, you can tell that this place was once an impressive building. At the hunting lodge we were entertained by period dance and refreshments. I was then asked by Letizia to follow her up into the building and I was robed as Prince Marino in full regalia. It was pretty funny to stand there and be dressed as if I was a noble from 1600. I then had to present myself as the prince. Not being the shy retiring type, this idea was not an issue. The best part... I got to keep the robes.

One of the best days of our journey was the day we met with my dad's first cousins. Up until about three months before the trip, I had not known about the son of my grandmother's half-sister Anna. His name is Nicola Di Paolo and out of the blue he contacted me on Facebook. I told him that I was coming, and he surprised us at the luncheon the previous Saturday. He told me that he wanted me to visit Torre Del Greco after the cemetery and that he would me us there in the morning.

Sitting in my 9th great-grandfather's chair Prince Marino II.

At the cemetery, he took us to the gravesite of my great-grandfather and his grandfather Nicola Piromallo. Interred in the same grave are his mother and father, his grandfather's aunt Emilia and Nicola's second wife. He also showed us the old Piromallo crypt, that my second great-grandfather Saverio Giovanni Piromallo sold, and Nicola explained that he liked women and gambling. In fact, my great-grandfather was illegitimate, so that explains a lot. Nicola tells me to get into the car with him and his daughter Nadia for the fifteen-minute ride to Torre Del Greco, and on the way we exchange family stories. I found out the one of my grandmother's brothers moved to Torre Del Greco and another eventually became an admiral, and his family is in Taranto. In fact, I am in contact with one of his sons and grandson.

Once we arrive at the apartment building, Nicola tells us to just wait one minute as he goes up one more flight of stairs and we hear him speaking in Italian to a woman. So, by now my curiosity is way up. As we get to the door, we are met by three women, two of which are my dad's first cousins and the other is the widow of his first cousin. WOW! I had no idea. I recall my father telling me some thirty-five years ago that he had a family in Torre Del Greco, but he never mentioned who they were.

So now, we are besieged with hugs and kisses and led into the living room where they start pulling out photos. My mom and dad's wedding, my grandparents forty-fifth anniversary, my cousins all with my grandmother's handwriting in Italian on the back.

Cugini

They, much to my amazement, start to tell me family stories from the 1960's. We then call Antoinetta's son who lives in San Diego.

In true style, we are then invited into the kitchen to have some homemade food followed by pastry and of course, limoncello. It was truly a wonderful surprise and I felt as if I knew them forever. It was sad to leave, and I would have loved to spend more time there, but we had to go as we had wine tasting and lunch scheduled at the Sorrentino Vineyard on the side of Vesuvius.

It was nice to get a break from the heat on the side of the volcano, and I must tell you that if you are ever in Naples, be sure to put the vineyard on your list. We had antipasto, fresh spaghetti in fresh tomato sauce and a light dessert to go with a tasting of five of their premium wines.

Back to Naples and of course, more food. The next two days were off days, and we went to Pompeii and took a long train ride to Scilla, which would be home for two nights.

The drive from Scilla to Montebello is about an hour. On the way, we stopped to view the mountain "ghost town" Pentedattilo, which is derived from the Greek language and means five fingers.

Our day in Montebello and Fossato turned out to be one of the more special days. Mostly due to my cousin Cinzia Piromallo (she and I on the second-floor balcony of Palazzo Piromallo in Montebello). Originally, I just planned to have a little side trip to Montebello just to see one of the ancestral homes. Instead, Cinzia, with the help of the leaders of several local associations made this one very special and memorable day. We were greeted by Mayor Maria Foti and welcomed by the association executives, Baron Cordopatri and other very special people that we will never forget.

Cinzia Piromallo / Bob Sorrentino

We were then brought to the first of my ancestors' homes in Montebello, which is still occupied. In the piazza outside the residence, we were met and entertained by Gino Neri, Angelo Roda and Pasquale Federico.

Much to my surprise, the current owner presented me with the key to open the door and allowed us upstairs to see the residence. Before leaving, the local florist presented my wife with a beautiful bouquet of roses colored blue and gold for the stemma of the Piromallo barons.

Our next stop was Fossato, a place up until a short while ago I did not know was a part of the Piromallo history. It was only a short ride, and everyone followed from Montebello. We arrived to renditions of the US and Italian National anthems and were led up a hill to the second Palazzo Piromallo. There, we found a spread of homemade eggplant parmigiana (courtesy of cousin Cinzia), cheese, ham, olives, bread and olive oil, cookies and of course wine.

After a bit, we were treated to a fashion show highlighted by my daughter Nicole, who was announced as the Contessa escorted by the Baron. Even Mayor Foti took part. After that, there was more singing, dancing and games. One game was the predecessor to bowling, where pins are set up in a diamond shape and you throw a type of bocce ball to knock them down. The secret, bounce, don't roll the ball. Another game, which is Internationally known, is to spin a top, then pick it up and place it on the palm of another and time how long it spins. We were told that one of the groups had it spinning for almost four minutes. No easy task.

What was truly special is that the wonderful people of Montebello and Fossato spent the entire day with us and treated as if we were their family. One resident even gave us a huge bottle of olive oil that she pressed herself.

Towards the end of the day, the current owner of the palazzo asked us if we would like to enter. He does not live in the building but in another home on the property. We were told that the lower level was once used for silkworm cultivation and the silk industry. It was nice to be able to go inside and one can only imagine the palazzo in its glory days.

What was very special was that the people planned this for months and spent the entire day with us. Words cannot express the feeling that we have for the people in these mountain top villages.

The following day, we took a short ferry ride from Reggio Calabria to the port of Messina in Sicily. From there, we made a two-hour drive to Cefalu. Neither my wife nor I have family from there, but we did meet up with a good friend, Francesco Curione, from 007 *With my friend Francesco Curione in Cefalu*

Italian Records. He and his friend Andrea spent the afternoon with us and took us to the beach, and the old Roman section where they would wash their clothes. They also introduced us to the Aperol Spritz, which became our drink of choice for the remainder of our trip.

I have to say that Sicily is beautiful and as you circumnavigate the island you have mountains on one side and the sea on the other. We did go to Sciacca a seaport and fishing town on the south-west part of the island, where my wife's grandparents were born. Another beautiful town!

Our final day had us back in Rome again, and we went to St. Peter's Basilica. I finally found the tomb of my 13th great-grandfather Pope Paul III, but we could not get right up to it as it appeared that they were preparing for a mass. But you can see it over my shoulder.

My final thoughts on our trip are that if you are planning a trip to Italy, be sure to do some research and find the homes of your ancestors, if you haven't already. There is nothing that will make you feel more connected to them, your roots and the people of Italy than walking the streets, going to a cafe, and meeting the people.

Records in the State Archives of Naples

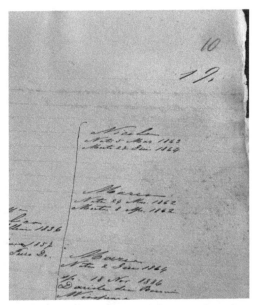

Handwritten Caracciolo Tree from the archives

San Francesco Caracciolo and Don Agostino

In a small chapel in the Duomo, my third great-grandparents names and stemma

Meeting the Mayor of Capracotta

Ancestral home Palazzo Caracciolo

Duomo

Crypt

Fun with Libatore

Dressed as Prince Marino

Scilla

Inside Palazzo Piromallo in Montebello

Church in Montebello

The Baron and Contessa

Torre Del Greco

Pentedattilo

Palazzo Piromallo Fossato

The Beautiful People of Montebello and Fossato

Village of Pentedattilo

Research Primer

By now you are probably wondering how I completed my research online. At the start I used mainly ancestry.com, however that is a site that you must pay to use, therefore I now recommend that people start with familysearch.org, especially if you are not that interested in finding distant cousins.

FamilySearch offers many tools, and they are the group that is filming and indexing records around the world. One drawback is that they do not offer the best charting tools, but you can always build these with third party software.

In my opinion, they make it easier than Ancestry to create a tree and search for records. They also assign a unique id's for everyone in the tree to make it quicker to recall that person.

Here's a small sample of my tree:

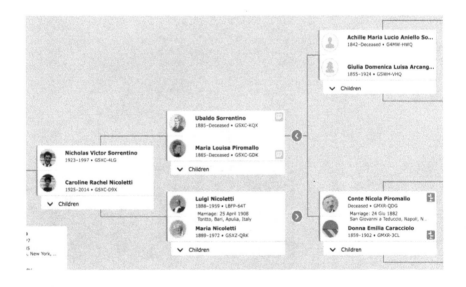

Notice the portrait photos. With Familysearch, you can take almost any family photo and crop one person to create a profile photo. You can see in my family tree (previous page), that I cut my mom and dad out of this photo to create their individual photos.

Another cool thing that they do with photos is "Compare-a-Face. This is me on my 27th birthday, and my 9th great-grandfather Prince Marino Caracciolo of Avellino. He died at the age of 47, I think we are probably close to the same age in this comparison.

Robert Sorrentino

36%

Prince Marino

9TH GREAT-GRANDFATHER

Here is the record of Baptism for my 4th great-grandfather, Joseph Mohr, born 1751 in Lucerne, Switzerland.

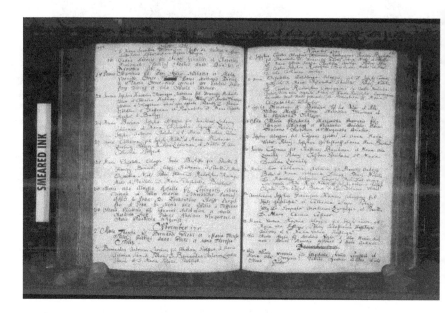

You can also upload a GED file from another source and create your tree on Familysearch.org. If you have the time, you can be part of the team the reviews and indexes records on a volunteer basis.

These are only a few of the resources available to you on Familysearch.org and I strongly suggest that you sign up for a free membership to explore all that they have to offer.

Many people have asked me how to find Italian birth records, do I have to pay etc. The best place to start in my opinion is the Italian Record site *Antenati*. This site, with the help of Familysearch.org has been digitizing the Italian Civil records that date back to 1809. While not every record is there, they constantly update, so you must check back often. What many people do not know, is that while all the records are in Italian, the search instructions are in English and Italian. Of course, the records are in Italian, but after a while you start to recognize the important information.

One thing to know when searching, is to use variations on a name. Many of the older records are difficult to read, and therefore the indices may be off. For example, my 2nd great grandmother's last name was Mohr. I found family under Mohr, Moher and Moler. Also, people may not always come from the exact place your grandparents told you. They may have told you Bari when it may have been a smaller town in Bari.

There are two ways to search records, by registry or by name.

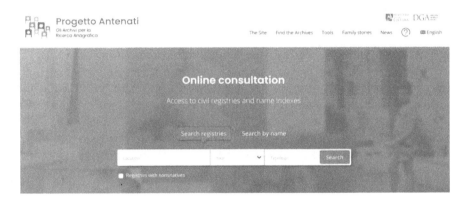

What is especially helpful is the drop down for locations and the slider for dates, it cuts down on the number of records returned.

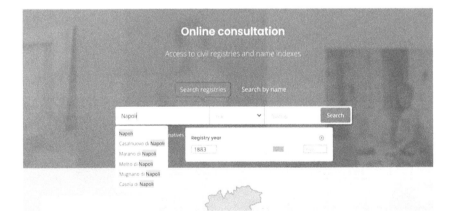

You also get a slider for dates, if you select the name option.

This is a search on my grandmother's maiden name PIROMALLO. Saverio, third from the top, is my great great-grandfather. Saverio's record is his birth, and you can see that they list his parents and birthdate. Using this, I was able to eventually find 4th cousins in Italy. What they also display in the left margin is all the people with this surname. You can also see the first names, locations and years for which records exist. This is a new feature that allows you to find other potential relatives very quickly.

Once you make your selection, the return this for verification. This is what you see once you open the record. To me the image appears clearer than on the old version. You'll also notice another new feature in the upper right-hand corner that allows you to adjust the image without sending to an editor.

The only thing that is not good, is that if you save the URL's of your records, they do not work in the new version, so you have to download your records again.

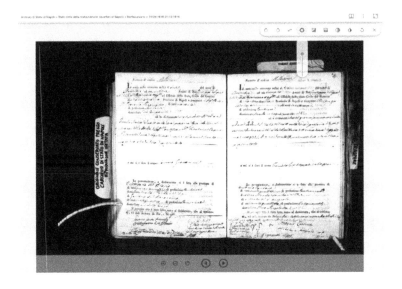

Dictionary

Ducat/Ducati - Gold coin of 3.545g of pure gold used primarily in European countries. First issued in Venice in the 13ᵗʰ Century. Today's value approximately $150.

HRE - Holy Roman Empire.

Scudi - gold coin in Spain and Italy.

Podesta - High civil office in northern and central Italy. Similar to a mayor or high magistrate.

Rettori or Rector - similar to a podesta.

Sindaco - Mayor.

King's Mouth - Speaks for the king.

Gonfoloniere - High prestigious office in Florence and Papal States.

Vicar - Basically and agent for a person, city or state.

Palantine Count - Ruled an area within a kingdom by decree of the monarch.

Natural Son/Daughter - Illegitimate child.

Antenati - record of Italian births/languages/deaths.

Guelphs - strong faction in medieval Italy that supported the power of the pope and city states in struggles against the German emperors and Ghibellines.

Ghibellines - faction in opposition to the Guelphs that supported the HRE against the pope.

Grand Camerario - Treasurer of the state.

Seneschal - the steward or major-domo of a medieval great house.

Condottiero - Italian mercenary captain usually contracted to popes or European monarchs from around 1350 to 1650.

Nobiliary Titles

The following nobility titles are an excerpt from historian Louis Mendola's website, "Italian Titles of Nobility": [4]

*"**Principe, Principessa**. (Prince, Princess). From the Latin princeps, meaning first, this is the highest Italian title of nobility, and also the title accorded members of the royal families. Many of Italy's noble princes, particularly in northern regions, are princes 'of the Holy Roman Empire,' and lack feudal territorial designations attached to their titles. Some southern princes descend from the most ancient medieval feudatories. In most cases, the holder of a princely title in Italy is the descendant of forebears who in antiquity were barons or counts, the family having been elevated through the nobiliary ranks over the centuries. Until the latter part of the nineteenth century, princes were addressed most formally as 'Your Excellency,' a form of address that may be compared, in this instance, to the British use of 'Your Grace' for a duke or duchess. The wife of a prince is a princess. The younger son of a prince, and the heir before succession to the title, is a nobile dei principi di (seat), namely a 'noble of the princes of' some place. Use of the honorific appellations don (lord) and donna (lady) for the son and daughter of a prince is obsolete except in formal documents issued by institutions that recognize Italian titular nobility. Princes and their consorts are most formally addressed verbally by title and territorial designation. The heraldic coronet of a noble prince is a jeweled circlet of gold surmounted by four visible pearls between five visible strawberry leaves. In most representations, the deep red tasseled cap is not rendered within the coronet.*

Duca, Duchessa. *(Duke, Duchess). Derived from the Latin dux, a military leader, this title originally was reserved to the sovereign rulers of important territories, such as the Duchy of Spoleto. Like princedoms, dukedoms are sometimes borne by nobles whose early medieval forebears were barons, enfeoffed knights or other feudatories. Like princes, dukes were formerly accorded the address 'Your Excellency.' The younger son of a duke, and the heir before succession to the title, is a nobile dei* *duchi di (seat), namely a 'noble of the dukes of' some place. Dukes and their consorts are most formally addressed verbally by title and territorial designation. The heraldic coronet of a duke is a jeweled circlet of gold surmounted by five visible strawberry leaves. Usually, the crimson tasseled cap is not rendered within the coronet.*

Marchese, Marchesa. *(Marquess, Marchioness). The term derives from the Old Italian marchio, referring to the man charged with guarding a march, or border territory, and the French marquis shares the same origin. The Marches region, which borders Umbria, is so-called because it was once such a territory. Some attribute the origin of this word to the Middle Latin marchisus, a prefect. Most marquessates are of modern foundation; one reads of few marchesi before the fifteenth century, and the title is quite rare even today. The younger son of a marquess, and the heir before succession to the title, is a nobile dei marchesi di (seat), namely a 'noble of the marquesses of' some place. Marquesses and their consorts are most formally addressed verbally by title and surname; since in Italy a woman usually continues to use her own father's surname even after marriage, a marchesa may bear a surname other than her husband's. The heraldic coronet of a marquess is a jeweled circlet of gold surmounted by three visible strawberry leaves, the central leaf flanked by two rows of three pearls each, supported by stems or set directly upon the rim.*

Conte, Contessa. *(Count, Countess). The word traces its origin from the Latin comes, for military companion. Comital territories were large in the eleventh century, but virtually indistinguishable from baronies by the fourteenth. For purposes of precedence, there is no contemporary distinction between a feudal count and a count palatine; the latter was usually a court officer who lacked a territorial designation attached to his title. It is noteworthy that conte is one of the few Italian titles sometimes, though rarely, inherited by all heirs male, depending on the terms set forth in the patent of creation; in Italy there are numerous counts of the Holy Roman Empire. The younger son of a count, and the heir before succession to the title, is a nobile dei conti di (seat), namely a 'noble of the counts of' some place. Counts and their consorts are most formally addressed verbally by title and surname. Counts palatine were created by certain sovereigns and by the Popes and usually bore no territorial designations attached to their surnames*

The heraldic coronet of a count is a jeweled circlet of gold surmounted by nine visible pearls, supported by stems or set directly upon the rim.

Visconte, Viscontessa. *(Viscount, Viscontess). Originally vice comes, for the attendant of a count, this is the rarest of the modern Italian nobiliary titles, almost unknown in some regions. The younger son of a viscount, and the heir before succession to the title, is a nobile dei visconti di (seat), namely a noble of the viscounts' of some place. The standard crest coronet of a viscount is a jeweled circlet of gold surmounted by five visible pearls, the middle and outer ones supported by stems, the remaining two rendered in a smaller diameter and set directly upon the rim.*

Barone, Baronessa. *(Baron, Baroness). The title is probably of Germanic origin; the Late Latin root being baro, but by the Middle Ages baronis was a title of nobility or, more often, a nobiliary rank employed in reference to holders of feudal property. Most seigneuries (see below) were eventually elevated to baronies. In the South, the most important medieval baronies were elevated to princedoms or dukedoms by the eighteenth century. Though often employed loosely in the remote past, the title barone was by 1800 established to be a creation or recognition resulting from royal prerogative, not an honorific privilege to be appropriated by any wealthy landholder. Heraldic regulation in the Kingdom of Italy further established that the sons of barons could no longer appropriate cavaliere as a courtesy title. Contrary to popular belief, barone probably is not the most frequent of the modern Italian noble titles; in Italy there are thought to be more counts than barons. The younger son of a baron, and the heir before succession to the title, is a nobile dei baroni di (seat), namely a noble of the barons of some place. The standard heraldic coronet of a baron is a jeweled circlet of gold surmounted by seven pearls, supported by stems or placed directly upon the rim. Italy has a number of 'incognito' barons, particularly in the regions of the former Papal State and Two Sicilies; for the most part these potential claimants descend from holders of tiny baronial estates who failed to petition for recognition after 1861.*

Signore *(seigneur). Originally a feudal lord, the title was introduced into Italy by the Franks and Normans. Formerly a minor title, the title is rarely used today because most signori bear greater titles by which they are commonly known, and* *because, in common parlance, signore has come to mean 'Mister.' Seigneuries were feudal lands, typically smaller than baronies, appertaining to certain lords, either as sub-fiefs attached to baronies or, more often, depending from the Crown directly. A signore might therefore owe fealty to a baron or directly to the king. This is the lowest title which carries a seat, and one could compare it to the English title lord of the manor (the origins of the Italian, English and French titles are Norman and traced to the eleventh century). As these noblemen bear a title which is no longer in use, though still mentioned in nobility directories, no particular crest coronet is displayed for this rank. In practice, a signore may display the coronet of an untitled nobleman (see below). In Piedmont, most holders of the former title Vassallo (see below) would be comparable to the signori of southern Italy.*

Vassallo *(vassal). This was the Piedmontese term for what Neapolitans and Sicilians referred to as a signore. The word was used until around 1800, and with the abolition of feudalism over the following decades most vassalli were recognized as baroni.*

Patrizio *(Patrician). The term obviously derives from that used to describe the aristocratic class of ancient Rome and described the urban patriciate of certain northern Italian cities and a few southern ones (Salerno, Messina). A patrizio is said to be 'of' a certain place, such as Venice or Florence, without it being his 'feudal' seat (patricians were an urban aristocracy confirmed by published lists). The rank is normally transmitted to heirs male general. According to legislation enacted by the Consulta Araldica, there is no feminine, but the daughter of a Patrizio might be said to be dei patrizi [surname], namely 'of the patricians [surname]. Patrizio is also the translation of the name Patrick; Patrizia is Patricia but is never used as a title. The crest coronet of a patrician is a simple jeweled circlet of gold.*

Nobile *(Untitled Nobleman). In the Dark Ages, local leaders known to their people were nobiliti, from the Latin nobilitas, meaning, appropriately, 'known.' The rank denotes some, but not all, aristocratic Italian families which lack titles. This class may be compared to the landed gentry of Great Britain. There are, strictly speaking, two kinds of nobili – the younger sons of titled nobles and male members of the aforementioned noble families in which there have never been titles. In the Kingdom* *of Sicily, the nobles of royal ('free') cities like Piazza Armerina and Calascibetta based their rank on their status as 'noble jurats' whose names were inscribed in the Mastra Nobile much as the patricians of larger cities were recognized. The crest coronet of a nobile is a jewelled circlet of gold surmounted by five pearls, supported by stems or set directly upon the rim.*

Cavaliere Ereditario *(Hereditary Knight Bachelor). This rank, usually transmitted by male primogeniture but sometimes to heirs male general, is quite similar to a British baronetcy but older. However, it does not, as is commonly believed, have any direct connection to the medieval rank of the enfeoffed knight. Most cavalieri ereditari descend from the younger sons of nobles or from historically untitled families ennobled with this form of knighthood in the fifteenth or sixteenth centuries in Sicily, Sardinia and some parts of mainland Italy. Writing in 1925, Francesco San Martino de Spucches speculated that, at least in theory, hundreds of Sicilians entitled to no other hereditary honour could lawfully succeed to particular hereditary knighthoods which were long-dormant for lack of claimants. Another category consists of the knights commander of legal patronage (giuspatronato) of the Constantinian Order; these were landholders who ceded large estates to that order of chivalry and in return bore a hereditary commandery transmitted by male primogeniture – the D'Elia family is a good example."[5]*

Saints

Saint Adalrich Alsace

Saint Arnulf of Metz (Patron Saint of Brewers)

Saint Begga Austrasia

Saint Clotilde of Burgundy

Saint Dagobert Merovigian

Saint Gertrude De Hamage

Saint Hedwig Andechs

Saint Imma Alemannia

Saint Irene of Hungary

Saint Irmina Von Oeren

Saint Kinga of Poland

Saint Ladislas of Hungary

Saint Lidmila of Bohemia

Saint Leopold Von Babenberg

Saint Louis IX Capet

Saint Margaret of Hungary

Saint Margaret of Wessex

Saint Mihail Vsvolodovich

Saint Olga of Kiev

Saint Raimond Deberenger

Saint Sigbert Merovigian

Saint Vladdimir Svyatoslavich

Saint Wenceslas II of Bohemia

Spanish Royalty

Male Line

Aragon

23rd   GG Alfonso II "The Chaste" King of Aragon (1157-1196) M. Sancia of Castile

23rd   GG Peter II King of Aragon (1174-1213) M. Lady Maria of Montpellier

22nd   GG James I "The Conqueror" (1208-1276) M. Yolanda of Hungary

21st   GG Peter III "The Great" King of Aragon and Sicily (1239-1285) M. Constance of Sicily

20th   GG James II "The Just" King of Aragon and Sicily (1267-1327) M. Blanche of Anjou

19th   GG Alfonso IV "The Benign" King of Aragon (1299-1336) M. Elenor of Castile

18th   GG Peter IV "The Ceremonious" King of Aragon (1319-1387)

18th   GG John I "The Abandoned" King of Aragon (1350-1396)

Barcelona

28th   GG Raimund I "The Cooked" King of Barcelona (1005-1035)

27th   GG Ferdinand I King of Barcelona (1016-1065)

26th   GG Raimund II King of Barcelona (1055-1082)

25th   GG Raimund III "The Great" King of Barcelona (1080-1131)

24th   GG Raymond IV King of Barcelona (1113-1182)

Castile and Leon

26th   GG - Alfonso VI King of Castile and Leon (1040-1109)

25th   GG - Alfonso VII King of Castile and Leon (1105-1157)

24th   GG - Fernando II King of Castile and Leon (1137-1188)

23rd GG - Alfonso IX "The Slobberer" King of Castile and Leon (1171-1230)

22nd GG - Ferdinand III "Saint" King of Castile and Leon (1199-1252)

21st GG - Alfonso X "The Wise" King of Castile and Leon (1221-1284)

20th GG - Sancho IV King of Castile and Leon (1258-1295)

Female Line

20th GG - Isabela of Aragon (1271-1336) Daughter of Peter III mother of Alfonso IV of Portugal

19th GG - Beatrice of Castile Infanta of Castile (1293-1359) mother of Alfonso IV of Portugal

Navarre

35th GG Inigo Arista (781-851)

34th GG Garcia I (810-882)

33rd GG Fotun "The One Eyed" (d 922)

32nd GG Sancho I (860-925)

31st GG Garcia III (919-970)

30th GG Sancho II (938-994)

29th GG Garcia II "The Trembler" (d 1000)

28th GG Sancho III "The Great" (991-1035)

26th GG Sancho V "The Great" (1042-1094)

French Royalty

29th   GG Hugh Capet King of the Franks (939-996)

29th   GG Robert II King of the Franks "The Pious" (972-1031)

28th   GG Henry I King of France (1008-1060)

27th   GG Philip I King of France (1053-1108)

26th   GG Louis VI "The Fat" King of France (1081-1137)

24th   GG Louis VII "The Younger" King of France (1119-1180)

23rd   GG Philip II "The August" King of France (1165-1223)

22nd   GG Louis VIII "The Lion" King of France (1183-1226)

21st   GG Louis IX "Saint" King of France (1214-1270)

20st   GG Phillip III" The Bold" King of France (1245-1285)

20th   GG Philip VI King of France (1293-1350)

19th   GG Jean II "The Good" King of France (1319-1364)

19th   GG Charles IV" The Simple" King of France (1270-1325)

Holy Roman Emperors

35th   GG Charlemagne (742-814)

35th   GG Lothar I (795-855)

34th   GG Louis I "The Pious" (778-840)

33rd   GG Charles II "The Bald" (823-877)

32nd   GG Henry I "The Fowler" (876-936)

31st   GG Otto I "The Great" (912-973)

30th   GG Otto II "The Red" (947-983)

29th   GG Otto III (980-1002)

29th   GG Conrad II (990-1039)

28th   GG Henry III "The Elder" (1017-1056)

28th   GG Agnes of Poitou (1025-1077)

28th   GG Lothar II (1075-11137)

27th   GG Henry IV (1050-1106)

25th   GG Frederick I "Barbarosa" (1122-1190)

23rd   GG Henry VI "The Cruel" (1165-1197)

22nd   GG Frederick II "The Fowler" (1194-1250)

22nd   GG Alfonso X of Castile "The Wise" (1221-1284)

21st   GG Rudolph I "The Great" (1218-1291)

British Royalty

Normans

27th   GG William I (1024-1097)

Plantagenet

26th   GG Henry I King of England (1069-1135)

25th   GG Holy Roman Empress, Queen of England* (1101-1169)

24th   GG Henry II King of England "Henry Curtmantle" (1133-1189)

23rd   GG John I King of England (1167-1213)

22nd   GG Henry III King of England (1207-1272)

21st   GG Edward I "Longshanks" King of England (1239-1307)

Kings of Wessex

39th   GG Egbert (771-839)

38th   GG Ethelwulf (d 858)

38th   GG Ethelred I (840-901)

Bohemian Royalty

32nd GG Borivoj I (852-889)

32nd GG Boleslav I "The Cruel" (935-972)

31st GG Vratislav I (877-921)

30th GG Oldrich II (966-1034)

29th GG Bretislaus I (1005-1055)

28th GG Vratislaus II (1035-1092)

25th GG Vladislaus II (1110-1175)

23rd GG Ottokar I (1155-1233)

22nd GG Wenceslas I (1205-1253)

21st GG Ottokar II (1253-1278)

20th GG Wenceslas III (1289-1306)

Portuguese Royalty

24th   GG Alfonso I "The Conqueror" (1110-1185)

23rd   GG Sancho I "The Fat, The Leprous" (1154-1211)

22nd   GG Alfonso II "The Conqueror" (1185-1223)

21st   GG Alfonso III "The Restorer" (1210-1279)

20th   GG Dionisio "The Farmer, The Troubadour" (1261-1325)

19th   GG Alfonso IV "The Brave" (1291-1357)

18th   GG Peter I "The Just, The Cruel" (1319-1387)

Russian Royalty

Princes of Novgorod

32nd   GG Rurik (830-879)

Princes of Kiev

31st   GG Igor (878-945)

31st   GG St. Olga (890-969)

30th   GG Sviatoslav (942-972)

29th   GG St. Vladamir (958-1015)

28th   GG Yaroslav "The Wise" (978-1054)

28th   GG Vselav "The Sorcerer" (1039-1101)

29th   GG Iziaslav I (1024-1078

27th   GG Vladimir II "He Who Fights Alone" (1053-1125)

26th   GG Mstislav "The Great" (1076-1132)

28th   GG Yaropolk II "The Wise" (1082-1139)

26th   GG Vsevolod "The Wise" (1084-1146)

The Royal and Noble Ancestry of Nicholas Victor Sorrentino

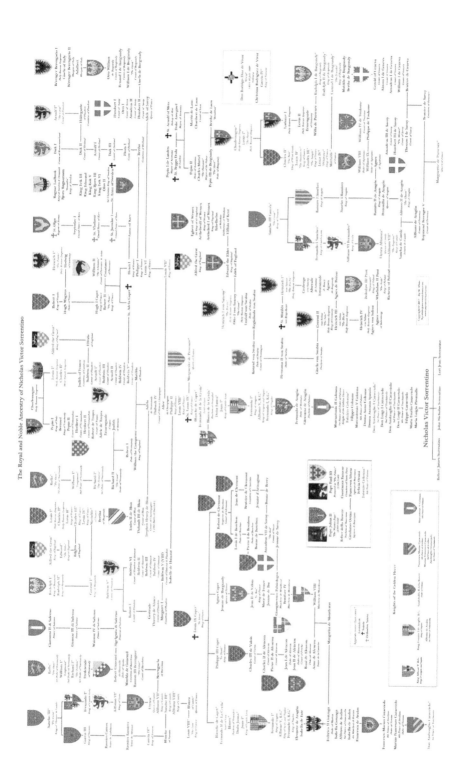

Nicholas Victor Sorrentino

[211]

Bibliography

"Afan De Rivera, Maria Francesca in 'Dizionario Biografico.'" in "Dizionario Biografico", 1960. https://www.treccani.it/enciclopedia/afan-de-rivera-maria-francesca_(Dizionario-Biografico).

"Alberto D'Este, Marquis of Ferrara." Wikipedia. Wikimedia Foundation, February 4, 2021. https://en.wikipedia.org/wiki/Alberto_d%27Este,_Marquis_of_Ferrara.

"Alberto I Della Scala." Alberto I della Scala. Accessed December 22, 2021. https://www.histouring.com/en/historical-figure/alberto-i-della-scala/.

"Avalos in 'Enciclopedia Italiana.'" in "Enciclopedia Italiana". Accessed December 20, 2021. https://www.treccani.it/enciclopedia/avalos_%28Enciclopedia-Italiana%29/.

"Bernabò Visconti." Military Wiki. Accessed December 22, 2021. https://military-history.famdom.com/wiki/Bernab%C3%B2_Visconti.

"Boniface III, Marquis of Montferrat." Wikipedia. Wikimedia Foundation, August 31, 2021. https://en.wikipedia.org/wiki/Boniface_III,_Marquis_of_Montferrat.

"Bonifacio Di Saluzzo." Wikipedia. Wikimedia Foundation, September 20, 2020. https://it.wikipedia.org/wiki/Bonifacio_di_Saluzzo.

Brunelli, Giampiero. "Spinola, Ambrogio in 'Dizionario Biografico.'" in "Dizionario Biografico", 2018. http://www.treccani.it/enciclopedia/ambrogio-spinola_%28Dizionario Biografico%29/

Brunelli, Giampiero. "Spinola, Filippo in 'Dizionario Biografico.'" in "Dizionario Biografico", 2018. http://www.treccani.it/enciclopedia/filippo-spinola_%28Dizionario-Biografico%29/.

"Caetani Nell'enciclopedia Treccani." nell'Enciclopedia Treccani. Accessed January 13, 2022. https://www.treccani.it/enciclopedia /caetani/

Caetani. Accessed January 13, 2022. http://www.genmareno-strum.com/pagine-lettere/letterac/Caetani/caetani-torre.htm.

Capece Piscicelli. Accessed December 21, 2021. http://www.genma-reno strum.com/pagine-lettere/leterac/capece/ CAPECE%20PISCICELLI.htm.

"Capéce Nell'enciclopedia Treccani." nell'Enciclopedia Treccani. Accessed December 21, 2021. http://www.treccani.it/enciclopedia/capece/.

Caracciolo Carafa e Linee Antiche dei Carafa. Accessed December 26, 2021. http://www.genmarenostrum.com/pagine-lettere/letterac/carafa/carafa1.htm.

"Caracciolo, Francesco Marino in 'Dizionario Biografico.'" in "Dizionario Biografico". Accessed December 19, 2021. http://www.treccani.it/enciclopedia/francesco-marino-caracciolo_(Dizionario-Biografico).

Carafa della Stadera. Accessed December 26, 2021. http://www.genmarenostrum.com/pagine-lettere/letterac/carafa/carafa-andria.htm.

Carafa di Policastro. Accessed December 26, 2021. http://www.genmarenostrum.com/pagine-lettere/letterac/carafa/carafa-policastro.htm.

"Caràcciolo, Giovanni, Detto Sergianni Nell'enciclopedia Treccani." nell'Enciclopedia Treccani. Accessed December 19, 2021. http://www.treccani.it/enciclopedia/caracciolo-giovanni-detto-sergianni/.

Colonna: Linee di Paliano, Zagarolo e Traetto. Accessed January 14, 2022. http://www.genmarenostrum.com/pagine-lettere/letterac/Colonna/colonna02.htm.

"Corréggio, Da Nell'enciclopedia Treccani." nell'Enciclopedia Treccani. Accessed January 15, 2022. https://www.treccani.it/enciclopedia/da-correggio.

Da correggio. Accessed January 15, 2022. http://www.genmarenostrum.com/pagine-lettere/letterac/da%20Correggio/correggio1.htm.

D'AQUINO: Linee Antiche. Accessed January 9, 2022. http://www.genmarenostrum.com/pagine-lettere/letterad/d'aquino/d'Aquino-antico.htm.

D'Aquino di Caramanico. Accessed January 9, 2022. http://www.genmarenostrum.com/pagine-lettere/letterad/d'aquino/Aquino%20di%20Caramanico.htm.

Del Balzo. Accessed December 23, 2021. http://www.genmarenostrum.com/pagine-lettere/letterab/del%20Balzo/DEL%20BALZO2.htm.

"Della Róvere Nell'enciclopedia Treccani." nell'Enciclopedia Treccani. Accessed December 22, 2021. http://www.treccani.it/enciclopedia/della-rovere/.

di Carpegna Faclonieri, Tomasso. "Montefeltro, Guido Di in 'Dizionario Biografico.'" in "Dizionario Biografico", 2012. http://www.treccani.it/enciclopedia/guido-di-montefeltro_(Dizionario-Biografico). Volume 76

di Carpegna Falconieri, Tomasso. "Montefeltro, Antonio Di in 'Dizionario Biografico.'" in "Dizionario Biografico", 2012. http://www.treccani.it/enciclopedia/antonio-di-montefeltro_(Dizionario-Biografico).

di Carpegna Falconieri, Tomasso. "Montefeltro, Federico Di in 'Dizionario Biografico.'" in "Dizionario Biografico", 2012. http://www.treccani.it/enciclopedia/federico-di-montefeltro_(Dizionario-Biografico).

di Carpegna Falconieri, Tomasso. "Montefeltro, Nolfo Di in 'Dizionario Biografico.'" in "Dizionario Biografico", 2012. http://www.treccani.it/enciclopedia/nolfo-di-montefeltro_(Dizionario-Biografico).

"D'OPPIDO." Ruffo linee antiche. Accessed January 4, 2022. http://www.genmarenostrum.com/pagine-lettere/letterar/Ruffo/Ruffo%20linee%20antiche.htm

"Ercole I D'este, Duke of Ferrara." Wikipedia. Wikimedia Foundation, September 27, 2021. https://en.wikipedia.org/wiki/Ercole_I_d%27Este,_Duke_of_Ferrara.

Fabbri, Pier Giovanni. "Malatesta, Andrea, Detto Malatesta in 'Dizionario Biografico.'" in "Dizionario Biografico", 2007.

https://www.treccani.it/enciclopedia/malatesta-andrea-detto-malatesta_(Dizionario-Biografico)/.

Falcioni, Anna. "Malatesta, Galeazzo in 'Dizionario Biografico.'" in "Dizionario Biografico", 2007. https://www.treccani.it/enciclopedia/galeazzo-malatesta_%28Dizionario-Biografico%29/.

Falcioni, Anna. "Malatesta, Galeotto in 'Dizionario Biografico.'" in "Dizionario Biografico", 2007. http://www.treccani.it/enciclopedia/galeotto-malatesta_(Dizionario-Biografico).

Famiglia Saluzzo. Accessed December 23, 2021. http://www.nobili-napoletani.it/Saluzzo.htm.

Famiglia Sambiase. Accessed January 27, 2022. http://www.nobili-napoletani.it/Sambiase.htm.

Famiglia Sanseverino. Accessed January 27, 2022. http://www.nobili-napoletani.it/Sanseverino.htm.

Famiglia Spinelli. Accessed December 17, 2021. http://www.nobili-napoletani.it/Spinelli.htm.

"Federico Da Montefeltro." Wikipedia. Wikimedia Foundation, October 5, 2021. https://en.wikipedia.org/wiki/Federico_da_Montefeltro.

"Federico Gonzaga Marchese e Poi Duca Di Mantova Marchese Di Monferrato Nell'enciclopedia Treccani." nell'Enciclopedia Treccani. Accessed December 18, 2021. https://www.treccani.it/enciclopedia/federico-gonzaga-marchese-e-poi-duca-di-mantova-marchese-di-monferrato/.

"Federico II Gonzaga, Duke of Mantua." Wikipedia. Wikimedia Foundation, November 13, 2021. https://en.wikipedia.org/wiki/Federico_II_Gonzaga,_Duke_of_Mantua.

"Ferdinand I of Naples." Wikipedia. Wikimedia Foundation, July 11, 2021. https://en.wikipedia.org/wiki/Ferdinand_I_of_Naples.

"Filangieri." FILANGERI AVELLINO. Accessed January 17, 2022. http://www.genmarenostrum.com/pagine-lettere/letteraf/FILANGERI/filangeri%20avellino.htm

"Filangièri Nell'enciclopedia Treccani." nell'Enciclopedia Treccani. Accessed January 17, 2022. https://www.treccani.it/enciclopedia/filangieri.

"Francesco I Da Carrara." Wikipedia. Wikimedia Foundation, March 2, 2021. https://en.wikipedia.org/wiki/Francesco_I_da_Carrara

"Francesco Maria I Della Rovere, Duke of Urbino." Wikipedia. Wikimedia Foundation, April 1, 2021. https://en.wikipedia.org/wiki/Francesco_Maria_I_della_Rovere,_Duke_of_Urbino.

"Francésco Gonzaga 4º Marchese Di Mantova Nell'enciclopedia Treccani." nell'Enciclopedia Treccani. Accessed December 18, 2021. https://www.treccani.it/enciclopedia/francesco-gonzaga-4%C2%BA-marchese-di-mantova/

Frettoni, Marina. "Della Rovere, Lavinia Feltria in 'Dizionario Biografico.'" in "Dizionario Biografico", 1989. http://www.treccani.it/enciclopedia/della-rovere-lavinia-feltria_(Dizionario-Biografico)

Gaetani dell'aquila D'ARAGONA 1. Accessed January 13, 2022. http://www.genmarenostrum.com/pagine-lettere/letterac/Caetani/gaetani1.htm

Gaetani dell'aquila D'ARAGONA 2. Accessed January 13, 2022. http://www.genmarenostrum.com/pagine-lettere/letterac/Caetani/gaetani2.HTM.

"Galeazzo I Visconti." Wikipedia. Wikimedia Foundation, August 7, 2021. https://en.wikipedia.org/wiki/Galeazzo_I_Visconti.

Gaudalupi, Francesco. "Palazzo Ducale - Martina Franca (TA)." Brundarte, May 6, 2017 http://www.brundarte.it/2017/02/05/palazzo-ducale-martina-franca-ta/

Gian Maria Varanini. "Della Scala, Alboino in 'Dizionario Biografico.'" in "Dizionario Biografico", 1989. http://www.treccani.it/enciclopedia/alboino-della-scala_(Dizionario-Biografico).

"Giovanni Della Rovere." Wikipedia. Wikimedia Foundation, February 15, 2021. https://en.wikipedia.org/wiki/Giovanni_della_Rovere.

"GONZAGA: SOVEREIGN LINE OF MANTUA." Gonzaga: Linea Sovrana di Mantova. Accessed December 18, 2021. http://www.genmarenostrum.com/pagine-lettere/letterag/gonzaga/GONZAGA2.htm

Grillo, Paolo. "Visconti, Matteo in 'Dizionario Biografico.'" in "Dizionario Biografico", 2020. http://www.treccani.it/enciclopedia/matteo-visconti_%28Dizionario-Biografico%29/

"Guidobaldo II Della Rovere, Duke of Urbino." Military Wiki. Accessed December 22, 2021. https://military-history.fandom.com/wiki/Guidobaldo_II_della_Rovere,_Duke_of_Urbino

I Caracciolo di Avellino. Accessed December 19, 2021. http://www.genmarenostrum.com/pagine-lettere/letterac/Caracciolo/caracciolo-avellino.htm.

I Caracciolo di Torchiarolo. Accessed December 16, 2021. http://www.genmarenostrum.com/pagine-lettere/letterac/Caracciolo/caracciolo-torchiarolo.htm.

I Caracciolo di Torchiarolo. Accessed December 19, 2021. http://www.genmarenostrum.com/pagine-lettere/letterac/Caracciolo/caracciolo-torchiarolo.htm.

I Caracciolo: Linee Antiche. Accessed December 19, 2021. http://www.genmarenostrum.com/pagine-lettere/letterac/Caracciolo/caracciolo1.htm.

"INDEX OF NOBLE FAMILIES OF THE MEDITERRANEAN." Indice Spinelli. Accessed December 17, 2021. http://www.genmarenostrum.com/pagine-lettere/letteras/spinelli/spinelli1.htm.

"Isabella D'este." Essay. In *Fornovo 1495: France's Bloody Fighting Retreat*. Westport, CT: Greenwood, 2005.

"Isabella D'ESTE." home. Accessed January 6, 2022. http://www.isabelladeste.org/isabella-deste.

"Jacopo II Da Carrara." Wikipedia. Wikimedia Foundation, February 5, 2021. https://en.wikipedia.org/wiki/Jacopo_II_da_Carrara.

"John II, Marquis of Montferrat." Wikipedia. Wikimedia Foundation, August 25, 2021. https://en.wikipedia.org/wiki/John_II,_Marquis_of_Montferrat.

Lazzarini, Isabella. "Paola Malatesta Gonzaga, Prima Marchesa Di Mantova in 'Dizionario Biografico.'" in "Dizionario Biografico", 2014. https://www.treccani.it/enciclopedia/paola-malatesta-gonzaga-prima-marchesa-di-mantova_%28Dizionario-Biografico%29/.

Lazzarini2001, Isabella. "Gonzaga, Guido in 'Dizionario Biografico.'" in "Dizionario Biografico", 2001. https://www.treccani.it/enciclopedia/guido-gonzaga_(Dizionario-Biografico).

Lecari, Andrea. "Spinola Doria, Paolo in 'Dizionario Biografico.'" in "Dizionario Biografico", 2018. http://www.treccani.it/enciclopedia/paolo-spinola-doria_%28Dizionario-Biografico%29/.

Libro d'oro della nobiltà mediterranea - livre d'or de la noblesse mediterranéenne- gotha of the Mediterranean nobility -Libro de Oro de la Nobleza del Mediterráneo. Accessed December 19, 2021. http://www.genmarenostrum.com/pagine-lettere/letterac/Caracciolo/anteprimacaracciolo.htm

"Libro D'Oro Gonzaga Ancient Lins." Gonzaga: Linee Antiche. Accessed December 18, 2021. http://www.genmarenostrum.com/pagine-lettere/letterag/gonzaga/GONZAGA1.htm.

"Ludovico II Gonzaga." Wikipedia. Wikimedia Foundation, February 6, 2021. https://en.wikipedia.org/wiki/Ludovico_II_Gonzaga.

"Malatesta Da Verucchio." Wikipedia. Wikimedia Foundation, August 17, 2021. https://en.wikipedia.org/wiki/Malatesta_da_Verucchio.

"Malatesta IV Malatesta." Wikipedia. Wikimedia Foundation, February 4, 2021. https://en.wikipedia.org/wiki/Malatesta_IV_Malatesta.

"Malatèsta Nell'enciclopedia Treccani." nell'Enciclopedia Treccani. Accessed December 30, 2021. http://www.treccani.it/enciclopedia/malatesta/.

"Malatèsta, Pandolfo I, Signore Di Rimini e Pesaro Nell'enciclopedia Treccani." nell'Enciclopedia Treccani. Accessed December 30,

2021. http://www.treccani.it/enciclopedia/malatesta-pandolfo-i-signore-di-rimini-e-pesaro.

"Manfred I of Saluzzo." Wikipedia. Wikimedia Foundation, May 2, 2020. https://en.wikipedia.org/wiki/Manfred_I_of_Saluzzo.

"Manfred IV of Saluzzo." Wikipedia. Wikimedia Foundation, December 19, 2021. https://en.wikipedia.org/wiki/Manfred_IV_of_Saluzzo.

"Manfrédo II Marchese Di Saluzzo Nell'Enciclopedia Treccani." nell'Enciclopedia Treccani. Accessed December 23, 2021. http://www.treccani.it/enciclopedia/manfredo-ii-marchese-di-saluzzo.

"Manfrédo III Marchese Di Saluzzo Nell'enciclopedia Treccani." nell'Enciclopedia Treccani. Accessed December 23, 2021. https://www.treccani.it/enciclopedia/manfredo-iii-marchese-di-saluzzo/.

"Margaret Paleologa." Wikipedia. Wikimedia Foundation, September 23, 2021. https://en.wikipedia.org/wiki/Margaret_Paleologa.

Marino Francesco Maria Caracciolo. Accessed December 19, 2021. https://clever-geek.imtqy.com/articles/7899099/index.html.

"Mastino II Della Scala." Wikipedia. Wikimedia Foundation, December 11, 2021. https://it.wikipedia.org/wiki/Mastino_II_della_Scala.

Mendola, Louis. Italian titles of nobility - a concise, Accurate Guide to nobiliary history, tradition and law in Italy until 1946 - facts, not fiction., 2015. http://regalis.com/nobletitles.htm.

Mendola, Louis. "Italian Titles of Nobility." Italian titles of nobility - a concise, Accurate Guide to nobiliary history, tradition and law in Italy until 1946 - facts, not fiction., 2015. http://regalis.com/nobletitles.htm.

"Montefeltro Nell'enciclopedia Treccani." nell'Enciclopedia Treccani. Accessed January 7, 2022. http://www.treccani.it/enciclopedia/montefeltro.

"Niccolò III D'Este, Marquis of Ferrara." Wikipedia. Wikimedia Foundation, January 5, 2022. https://en.wikipedia.org/wiki/Niccol%C3%B2_III_d%27Este,_Marquis_of_Ferrara.

Origini della Dinastia Colonna : Tuscolani. Accessed January 14, 2022. http://www.genmarenostrum.com/pagine-lettere/letterac/Colonna/conti%20di%20tuscolo.htm.

Origini della Dinastia Colonna : Tuscolani. Accessed January 14, 2022. http://www.genmarenostrum.com/pagine-lettere/letterac/Colonna/conti%20di%20tuscolo.htm.

"Orsini Del Balzo, Raimondo Nell'enciclopedia Treccani." nell'Enciclopedia Treccani. Accessed December 23, 2021. https://www.treccani.it/enciclopedia/orsini-del-balzo-raimondo/.

"Orsini Nell'enciclopedia Treccani." nell'Enciclopedia Treccani. Accessed January 23, 2022. https://www.treccani.it/enciclopedia/orsini/.

"Orsini, Nicola, Conte Di Nola Nell'enciclopedia Treccani." nell'Enciclopedia Treccani. Accessed December 23, 2021. http://www.treccani.it/enciclopedia/orsini-nicola-conte-di-nola/.

Orsini. Accessed January 23, 2022. http://www.genmarenostrum.com/pagine-lettere/letterao/Orsini/ORSINI-BRACCIANO.htm.

Orsini. Accessed January 23, 2022. http://www.genmarenostrum.com/pagine-lettere/letterao/Orsini/orsini-gravina.htm.

Orsini. Accessed January 23, 2022. http://www.genmarenostrum.com/pagine-lettere/letterao/Orsini/orsini.htm.

"Palaeologus-Montferrat." Wikipedia. Wikimedia Foundation, September 30, 2021. https://en.wikipedia.org/wiki/Palaeologus-Montferrat.

Pignatelli, Ferdinando I. Accessed January 4, 2022. https://clever-geek.imtqy.com/articles/6125911/.

"Pignatèlli Nell'enciclopedia Treccani." nell'Enciclopedia Treccani. Accessed January 4, 2022. http://www.treccani.it/enciclopedia/pignatelli/.

"Pignatèlli, Ettore Nell'Enciclopedia Treccani." nell'Enciclopedia Treccani. Accessed January 4, 2022. http://www.treccani.it/enciclopedia/ettore-pignatelli.

"Pignatèlli, Fabrizio Nell'enciclopedia Treccani." nell'Enciclopedia Treccani. Accessed January 4, 2022. http://www.treccani.it/enciclopedia/fabrizio-pignatelli.

Pontieri, Ernesto. "Del Balzo in 'Enciclopedia Italiana.'" in "Enciclopedia Italiana", 1931. http://www.treccani.it/enciclopedia/del-balzo_%28Enciclopedia-Italiana%29/.

Quazza, Romolo. "Federico Gonzaga, Terzo Marchese Di Mantova in 'Enciclopedia Italiana.'" in "Enciclopedia Italiana", 1932. ttps://www.treccani.it/enciclopedia/federico-gonzaga-terzo-marchese-di-mantova_%28Enciclopedia-Italiana%29/.

Ruffo di Bagnara E Castelcicala. Accessed January 4, 2022. http://www.genmarenostrum.com/pagine-lettere/letterar/Ruffo/Ruffo%20di%20bagnara.htm.

"Ruffo Nell'enciclopedia Treccani." nell'Enciclopedia Treccani. Accessed January 4, 2022. http://www.treccani.it/enciclopedia/ruffo/.

Sambiase. Accessed January 27, 2022. http://www.genmarenostrum.com/pagine-lettere/letteras/sambiase.htm.

Sanseverino. Accessed January 27, 2022. http://www.genmarenostrum.com/pagine-lettere/letteras/SANSEVERINO/SANSEVERINO2.htm.

Settia, Aldo. "Giangiacomo Paleologo, Marchese Di Monferrato in 'Dizionario Biografico.'" in "Dizionario Biografico", 2000. https://www.treccani.it/enciclopedia/giangiacomo-paleologo-marchese-di-monferrato_%28Dizionario-Biografico%29/.

"Sfòrza, Alessandro, Signore Di Pesaro Nell'enciclopedia Treccani." nell'Enciclopedia Treccani. Accessed January 28, 2022. https://www.treccani.it/enciclopedia/sforza-alessandro-signore-di-pesaro/.

"SFÒRZA, Muzio Attendolo Detto Lo Nell'Enciclopedia Treccani." nell'Enciclopedia Treccani. Accessed January 28, 2022. https://www.treccani.it/enciclopedia/muzio-attendolo-detto-lo-sforza/.

"Stefano Visconti." Wikipedia. Wikimedia Foundation, October 3, 2021. https://en.wikipedia.org/wiki/Stefano_Visconti.

"Theodore I, Marquis of Montferrat." Wikipedia. Wikimedia Foundation, November 25, 2021. https://en.wikipedia.org/wiki/Theodore_I,_Marquis_of_Montferrat.

"Thomas I of Saluzzo." Wikipedia. Wikimedia Foundation, November 29, 2020. https://en.wikipedia.org/wiki/Thomas_I_of_Saluzzo.

"Thomas II." Wikipedia. Wikimedia Foundation, June 4, 2018. https://en.wikipedia.org/wiki/Thomas_II.

"Thomas III." Wikipedia. Wikimedia Foundation, January 11, 2019. https://en.wikipedia.org/wiki/Thomas_III.

Trastamara. Accessed December 21, 2021. http://www.genmarenostrum.com/pagine-lettere/letterat/trastamara.htm.

Viola, Massimo. "Love in the Renaissance - the Secret Story between Lucrezia Borgia and Francesco Gonzaga." HubPages. HubPages, February 12, 2021. https://discover.hubpages.com/education/Love-in-the-Renaissance-The-Secret-Story-between-Lucrezia-Borgia-and-Francesco-Gonzaga.

"William IX, Marquis of Montferrat." Wikipedia. Wikimedia Foundation, August 21, 2021. https://en.wikipedia.org/wiki/William_IX,_Marquis_of_Montferrat.

Zurlo e Capece Zurlo. Accessed December 21, 2021. http://www.genmarenostrum.com/pagine-lettere/letterac/capece/zurlo_e_capece_zurlo.htm.

"Ávalos, Íñigo d' Nell'enciclopedia Treccani." nell'Enciclopedia Treccani. Accessed December 20, 2021. https://www.treccani.it/enciclopedia/inigo-d-avalos/.

"Òbizzo III Marchese D'Este Nell'Enciclopedia Treccani." nell'Enciclopedia Treccani. Accessed January 6, 2022. http://www.treccani.it/enciclopedia/obizzo-iii-marchese-d-este.

Endnotes

Caracciolo

[1] Libro d'oro della nobiltà mediterranea - livre d'or de la noblesse mediterranéenne- gotha of the Mediterranean nobility -Libro de Oro de la Nobleza del Mediterráneo. Accessed December 19, 2021. http://www.genmarenostrum.com /pagine-lettere/letterac/Caracciolo /anteprimacaracciolo.htm.

[2] Caracciolo: Linee Antiche. Accessed December 19, 2021. http://www.genmarenostrum.com/pagine-lettere/letterac/Caracciolo/caracciolo1.htm.

[3] Caracciolo di Torchiarolo. Accessed December 19, 2021. http://www.genmare nostrum.com/pagine-lettere/letterac/Caracciolo/caracciolo-torchiarolo.htm.

[4] Caracciolo di Avellino. Accessed December 19, 2021. http://www.genmare nostrum.com/pagine-lettere/letterac/Caracciolo/caracciolo-avellino.htm.

[5] "Caracciolo, Francesco Marino in 'Dizionario Biografico,'" in "Dizionario Biografico", accessed December 19, 2021, http://www.treccani.it/enciclopedia /francesco-marino-caracciolo_(Dizionario-Biografico).

[6] Marino Francesco Maria Caracciolo. Accessed December 19, 2021. https:// clever-geek.imtqy.com/articles/7899099/index.htm.

[7] Caracciolo di Torchiarolo. Accessed December 19, 2021. http://www.genmare nostrum.com/pagine-lettere/letterac/Caracciolo/caracciolo-torchiarolo.htm.

[8] "Caràcciolo, Giovanni, Detto Sergianni Nell'enciclopedia Treccani." nell'Enciclopedia Treccani. Accessed December 19, 2021. http:// www.treccani.it/enciclopedia/caracciolo-giovanni-detto-sergianni/.

D'Aquino

[9] D'AQUINO : Linee Antiche. Accessed January 9, 2022. http:// www.genmarenostrum.com/pagine-lettere/letterad/d'aquino/d'Aquino-antico.htm.

[10] D'Aquino di Caramanico. Accessed January 9, 2022. http://www.genmare nostrum.com/pagine-lettere/letterad/d'aquino/Aquino%20di%20 Caramanico.htm.

D'Avalos

[1] "Avalos in 'Enciclopedia Italiana.'" in "Enciclopedia Italiana". Accessed December 20, 2021. https://www.treccani.it/enciclopedia/avalos_%28 Enciclopedia-Italiana%29/.

[2] "Ávalos, Íñigo d' Nell'enciclopedia Treccani." nell'Enciclopedia Treccani. Accessed December 20, 2021. https://www.treccani.it/enciclopedia/inigo-d-avalos/.

[3] "Ávalos, Íñigo d' Nell'enciclopedia Treccani." nell'Enciclopedia Treccani. Accessed December 20, 2021. https://www.treccani.it/enciclopedia/inigo-d-avalos/.

D'Aragona

1] Britannica, The Editors of Encyclopaedia. "Ferdinand I". Encyclopedia Britannica, 29 Mar. 2021, https://www.britannica.com/biography/Ferdinand-I-king-of-Aragon. Accessed 3 December 2021.

[2] Trastamara. Accessed December 21, 2021. http://www.genmarenostrum.com/pagine-lettere/letterat/trastamara.htm.

[3] Sáez, Emilio. "Alfonso V". Encyclopedia Britannica, 23 Jun. 2021, https://www.britannica.com/biography/Alfonso-V-king-of-Aragon-and-Naples. Accessed 3 December 2021.

[4] Britannica, The Editors of Encyclopaedia. "Ferdinand I". Encyclopedia Britannica, 21 Jan. 2021, https://www.britannica.com/biography/Ferdinand-I-king-of-Naples. Accessed 3 December 2021.

[5] Trastamara. Accessed December 21, 2021. http://www.genmarenostrum.com/pagine-lettere/letterat/trastamara.htm.

[6] Wikipedia contributors, "Ferdinand I of Naples," *Wikipedia, The Free Encyclopedia,* https://en.wikipedia.org/w/index.php?title=Ferdinand_I_of_Naples&oldid=1064465393 (accessed January 10, 2022).

[7] Trastamara. Accessed December 21, 2021. http://www.genmarenostrum.com/pagine-lettere/letterat/trastamara.htm.

[8] Wikipedia contributors, "Eleanor of Naples, Duchess of Ferrara," *Wikipedia, The Free Encyclopedia,* https://en.wikipedia.org/w/index.php?title=Eleanor_of_Naples,_Duchess_of_Ferrara&oldid=1005176857 (accessed January 10, 2022).

d'Este

[1] "Isabella D'este." Essay. In Fornovo 1495: France's Bloody Fighting Retreat. Westport, CT: Greenwood, 2005.

[2] "Isabella D'ESTE." Accessed January 6, 2022. http://www.isabelladeste.org/isabella-deste.

[3] Wikipedia contributors, "Ercole I d'Este, Duke of Ferrara," Wikipedia, The Free Encyclopedia, https://en.wikipedia.org/w/index.php?title=Ercole_I_d%27Este,_Duke_of_Ferrara&oldid=1046774632 (accessed January 11, 2022).

[4] Wikipedia contributors, "Niccolò III d'Este, Marquis of Ferrara," Wikipedia, The Free Encyclopedia, https://en.wikipedia.org/w/index.php?title=Niccol%C3%B2_III_d%27Este,_Marquis_of_Ferrara&oldid=1063830244 (accessed January 11, 2022).

[5] Wikipedia contributors, "Alberto d'Este, Marquis of Ferrara," Wikipedia, The Free Encyclopedia, https://en.wikipedia.org/w/index.php?title=Alberto_d%27Este,_Marquis_of_Ferrara&oldid=1004794638 (accessed January 11, 2022).

[6] Ò"bizzo III Marchese D'Este Nell'Enciclopedia Treccani." nell'Enciclopedia Treccani. Accessed January 6, 2022. http://www.treccani.it/enciclopedia/obizzo-iii-marchese-d-este.

Capece
[1] "Capéce Nell'enciclopedia Treccani." nell'Enciclopedia Treccani. Accessed December 21, 2021. http://www.treccani.it/enciclopedia/capece/.

[2] Capece Piscicelli. Accessed December 21, 2021. http://www.genmarenostrum.com/pagine-lettere/letterac/capece/CAPECE%20PISCICELLI.htm.

[3] Zurlo e Capece Zurlo. Accessed December 21, 2021. http://www.genmarenostrum.com/pagine-lettere/letterac/capece/zurlo_e_capece_zurlo.htm

Carafa
[1] Caracciolo Carafa e Linee Antiche dei Carafa. Accessed December 26, 2021. http://www.genmarenostrum.com/pagine-lettere/letterac/carafa/carafa1.htm.

[2] Carafa di Policastro. Accessed December 26, 2021. http://www.genmarenostrum.com/pagine-lettere/letterac/carafa/carafa-policastro.htm.

[3] Carafa della Stadera. Accessed December 26, 2021. http://www.genmarenostrum.com/pagine-lettere/letterac/carafa/carafa-andria.htm.

Carrara

[11] Britannica, The Editors of Encyclopaedia. "Carrara Family". Encyclopedia Britannica, 26 Jul. 2007, https://www.britannica.com/topic/Carrara-family. Accessed 2 December 2021.

[12] Wikipedia contributors. Jacopo II da Carrara [Internet]. Wikipedia, The Free Encyclopedia; 2022 Jan 1, 13:01 UTC [cited 2022 Jan 12]. Available from: https://en.wikipedia.org/w/index.php?title=Jacopo_II_da_Carrara&oldid=1063137931.

[13] Wikipedia contributors, "Francesco I da Carrara," *Wikipedia, The Free Encyclopedia,* https://en.wikipedia.org/w/index.php?title=Francesco_I_da_Carrara&oldid=1009847769 (accessed January 12, 2022).

Caetani

[1] "Caetani Nell'enciclopedia Treccani." nell'Enciclopedia Treccani. Accessed January 13, 2022. https://www.treccani.it/enciclopedia/caetani/.

[2] Gaetani dell'aquila D'ARAGONA 1. Accessed January 13, 2022. http://www.genmarenostrum.com/pagine-lettere/letterac/Caetani/gaetani1.htm.

[3] Caetani. Accessed January 13, 2022. http://www.genmarenostrum.com/pagine-lettere/letterac/Caetani/caetani-torre.htm.

[4] Gaetani dell'aquila D'ARAGONA 2. Accessed January 13, 2022. http://www.genmarenostrum.com/pagine-lettere/letterac/Caetani/gaetani2.HTM.

Colonna

[1] Origini della Dinastia Colonna: Tuscolani. Accessed January 14, 2022. http://www.genmarenostrum.com/pagine-lettere/letterac/Colonna/conti%20di%20tuscolo.htm.

[2] Colonna: Linee di Paliano, Zagarolo e Traetto. Accessed January 14, 2022. http://www.genmarenostrum.com/pagine-lettere/letterac/Colonna/colonna02.htm.

[3] Origini della Dinastia Colonna: Tuscolani. Accessed January 14, 2022. http://www.genmarenostrum.com/pagine-lettere/letterac/Colonna/conti%20di%20tuscolo.htm.

Coreggio

[1] "Corréggio, Da Nell'enciclopedia Treccani." nell'Enciclopedia Treccani. Accessed January 15, 2022. https://www.treccani.it/enciclopedia/da-correggio.

[2] Da correggio. Accessed January 15, 2022. http://www.genma-renostrum.com/pagine-lettere/letterac/da%20Correggio/correg-gio1.htm.

Del Balzo
[1] Pontieri, Ernesto. "Del Balzo in 'Enciclopedia Italiana.'" in "Enciclopedia Italiana", 1931. http://www.treccani.it/enciclopedia/del-balzo_%28Enciclo-pedia-Italiana%29/.

[2] Del Balzo. Accessed December 23, 2021. http://www.genmarenos-trum.com/pagine-lettere/letterab/del%20Balzo/DEL%20BALZO2.htm.

[3] "Orsini, Nicola, Conte Di Nola Nell'enciclopedia Treccani." nell'Enciclope-dia Treccani. Accessed December 23, 2021. http://www.treccani.it/enciclope-dia/orsini-nicola-conte-di-nola/.

[4] "Orsini Del Balzo, Raimondo Nell'enciclopedia Treccani." nell'Enciclope-dia Treccani. Accessed December 23, 2021. https://www.treccani.it/enciclo-pedia/orsini-del-balzo-raimondo/.

Della Rovere
[1] "Della Róvere Nell'enciclopedia Treccani." nell'Enciclopedia Treccani. Accessed December 22, 2021. http://www.treccani.it/enciclopedia/della-rovere/.

[2] Frettoni, Marina. "Della Rovere, Lavinia Feltria in 'Dizionario Biografico.'" in "Dizionario Biografico", 1989. http://www.treccani.it/enciclopedia/della-rovere-lavinia-feltria_(Dizionario-Biografico).

[3] "Guidobaldo II Della Rovere, Duke of Urbino." Military Wiki. Accessed December 22, 2021. https://military-history.fanom.com/wiki/Guidobaldo_II_della_Rovere,_Duke_of_Urbino.

[4] "Francesco Maria I Della Rovere, Duke of Urbino." Wikipedia. Wikimedia Foundation, April 1, 2021. https://en.wikipedia.org/wiki/Francesco_Ma-ria_I_della_Rovere,_Duke_of_Urbino.

[5] "Giovanni Della Rovere." Wikipedia. Wikimedia Foundation, February 15, 2021. https://en.wikipedia.org/wiki/Giovanni_della_Rovere.

Della Scala
[1] "Alberto I Della Scala." Alberto I della Scala. Accessed December 22, 2021. https://www.histouring.com/en/historical-figure/alberto-i-della-scala/.

[2] Gian Maria Varanini. "Della Scala, Alboino in 'Dizionario Biografico.'" in "Dizionario Biografico", 1989. http://www.treccani.it/enciclopedia/alboino-della-scala_(Dizionario-Biografico).

[3] Wikipedia contributors, "Mastino II della Scala," *Wikipedia, The Free Encyclopedia*, https://en.wikipedia.org/w/index.php?title=Mastino_II_della_Scala&oldid=1044187358 (accessed January 17, 2022).

Farnese
[1] Murphy, Francis Xavier. "Paul III." Encyclopedia Britannica, November 6, 2021. https://www.britannica.com/biography/Paul-III.

[2] treccani.it/enciclopedia/pier-luigi-farnese-duca-di-parma-e-piacenza

Filangieri
[1] "Filangièri Nell'enciclopedia Treccani." nell'Enciclopedia Treccani. Accessed January 17, 2022. https://www.treccani.it/enciclopedia/filangieri.

[2] "Filangieri." FILANGERI AVELLINO. Accessed January 17, 2022. http://www.genmarenostrum.com/pagine-lettere/letteraf/FILANGERI/filangeri%20avellino.htm.

Gonzaga
[1] Britannica, The Editors of Encyclopaedia. "Gonzaga Dynasty". Encyclopedia Britannica, 9 Feb. 2012, https://www.britannica.com/topic/Gonzaga-dynasty. Accessed 4 December 2021.

[2] genmarenostrum.com/pagine-lettere/letterag/gonzaga/GONZAGA1.htm

[3] treccani.it/enciclopedia/guido-gonzaga_(Dizionario-Biografico)/

[4] Wikipedia contributors, "Ludovico II Gonzaga," *Wikipedia, The Free Encyclopedia*, https://en.wikipedia.org/w/index.php?title=Ludovico_II_Gonzaga&oldid=1005166247 (accessed January 18, 2022).

[5] genmarenostrum.com/pagine-lettere/letterag/gonzaga/GONZAGA2.htm

[6] treccani.it/enciclopedia/federico-gonzaga-terzo-marchese-di-mantova_%28Enciclopedia-Italiana%29/

[7] www.treccani.it/enciclopedia/francesco-ii-gonzaga-marchese-di-mantova_(Dizionario-Biografico)

[8] discover.hubpages.com/education/Love-in-the-Renaissance-The-Secret-Story-between-Lucrezia-Borgia-and-Francesco-Gonzaga

[9] Wikipedia contributors, "Federico II Gonzaga, Duke of Mantua," *Wikipedia, The Free Encyclopedia,* https://en.wikipedia.org/w/index.php?title=Federico_II_Gonzaga,_Duke_of_Mantua&oldid=1064371407 (accessed January 18, 2022).

[10] treccani.it/enciclopedia/federico-gonzaga-marchese-e-poi-duca-di-mantova-marchese-di-monferrato/

Malatesta

[1] "Malatèsta Nell'enciclopedia Treccani." nell'Enciclopedia Treccani. Accessed December 30, 2021. http://www.treccani.it/enciclopedia/malatesta/

[2]Wikipedia contributors, "Malatesta da Verucchio," *Wikipedia, The Free Encyclopedia,* https://en.wikipedia.org/w/index.php?title=Malatesta_da_Verucchio&oldid=1064597974 (accessed January 21, 2022).

[3] "Malatèsta, Pandolfo I, Signore Di Rimini e Pesaro Nell'enciclopedia Treccani." nell'Enciclopedia Treccani. Accessed December 30, 2021. http://www.treccani.it/enciclopedia/malatesta-pandolfo-i-signore-di-rimini-e-pesaro.

[4] Falcioni, Anna. "Malatesta, Galeotto in 'Dizionario Biografico.'" in "Dizionario Biografico", 2007. http://www.treccani.it/enciclopedia/galeotto-malatesta_(Dizionario-Biografico).

[5] Fabbri, Pier Giovanni. "Malatesta, Andrea, Detto Malatesta in 'Dizionario Biografico.'" in "Dizionario Biografico", 2007. https://www.treccani.it/enciclopedia/malatesta-andrea-detto-malatesta_(Dizionario-Biografico)/.

[6] Lazzarini, Isabella. "Paola Malatesta Gonzaga, Prima Marchesa Di Mantova in 'Dizionario Biografico.'" in "Dizionario Biografico", 2014. https://www.treccani.it/enciclopedia/paola-malatesta-gonzaga-prima-marchesa-di-mantova_%28Dizionario-Biografico%29/.

[7] Falcioni, Anna. "Malatesta, Galeazzo in 'Dizionario Biografico.'" in "Dizionario Biografico", 2007. https://www.treccani.it/enciclopedia/galeazzo-malatesta_%28Dizionario-Biografico%29/.

[8] Wikipedia contributors, "Malatesta IV Malatesta," *Wikipedia, The Free Encyclopedia,* https://en.wikipedia.org/w/index.php?title=Malatesta_IV_Malatesta&oldid=1063134185 (accessed January 21, 2022).

Montefeltro

[1] "Montefeltro Nell'enciclopedia Treccani." nell'Enciclopedia Treccani. Accessed January 7, 2022. http://www.treccani.it/enciclopedia/montefeltro.

[2] di Carpegna Faclonieri, Tommaso. "Montefeltro, Guido Di in 'Dizionario Biografico.'" in "Dizionario Biografico", 2012. http://www.treccani.it/enciclopedia/guido-di-montefeltro_(Dizionario-Biografico).

[3] di Carpegna Falconieri, Tommaso. "Montefeltro, Federico Di in 'Dizionario Biografico.'" in "Dizionario Biografico", 2012. http://www.treccani.it/enciclopedia/federico-di-montefeltro_(Dizionario-Biografico).

[4] di Carpegna Falconieri, Tommaso. "Montefeltro, Nolfo Di in 'Dizionario Biografico.'" in "Dizionario Biografico", 2012. http://www.treccani.it/enciclopedia/nolfo-di-montefeltro_(Dizionario-Biografico).

[5] di Carpegna Falconieri, Tommaso. "Montefeltro, Antonio Di in 'Dizionario Biografico.'" in "Dizionario Biografico", 2012. http://www.treccani.it/enciclopedia/antonio-di-montefeltro_(Dizionario-Biografico).

[6] Wikipedia contributors, "Federico da Montefeltro," *Wikipedia, The Free Encyclopedia,* https://en.wikipedia.org/w/index.php?title=Federico_da_Montefeltro&oldid=1048383756 (accessed January 21, 2022).

Montferrat
[1] Wikipedia contributors, "Palaeologus-Montferrat," *Wikipedia, The Free Encyclopedia,* https://en.wikipedia.org/w/index.php?title=Palaeologus-Montferrat&oldid=1047362944 (accessed January 22, 2022).

[2] Wikipedia contributors, "Theodore I, Marquis of Montferrat," *Wikipedia, The Free Encyclopedia,* https://en.wikipedia.org/w/index.php?title=Theodore_I,_Marquis_of_Montferrat&oldid=1057082953 (accessed January 22, 2022).

[3] Wikipedia contributors, "John II, Marquis of Montferrat," *Wikipedia, The Free Encyclopedia,* https://en.wikipedia.org/w/index.php?title=John_II,_Marquis_of_Montferrat&oldid=1040547941 (accessed January 22, 2022).

[4] Settia, Aldo. "Giangiacomo Paleologo, Marchese Di Monferrato in 'Dizionario Biografico.'" in "Dizionario Biografico", 2000. https://www.treccani.it/enciclopedia/giangiacomo-paleologo-marchese-di-monferrato_%28Dizionario-Biografico%29/.

[5] Wikipedia contributors, "Boniface III, Marquis of Montferrat," *Wikipedia, The Free Encyclopedia,* https://en.wikipedia.org/w/index.php?title=Boniface_III,_Marquis_of_Montferrat&oldid=1066168589 (accessed January 22, 2022).

[6] Wikipedia contributors, "William IX, Marquis of Montferrat," *Wikipedia, The Free Encyclopedia,* https://en.wikipedia.org/w/index.php?title=William_IX,_Marquis_of_Montferrat&oldid=1039902496 (accessed January 22, 2022).

[7] Wikipedia contributors, "Margaret Paleologa," *Wikipedia, The Free Encyclopedia,* https://en.wikipedia.org/w/index.php?title=Margaret_Paleologa&oldid=1046050303 (accessed January 22, 2022).

Orsini
[1] "Orsini Nell'enciclopedia Treccani." nell'Enciclopedia Treccani. Accessed January 23, 2022. https://www.treccani.it/enciclopedia/orsini/.

[2] Orsini. Accessed January 23, 2022. http://www.genmarenostrum.com/pagine-lettere/letterao/Orsini/orsini.htm.

[3] Orsini. Accessed January 23, 2022. http://www.genmarenostrum.com/pagine-lettere/letterao/Orsini/ORSINI-BRACCIANO.htm.

[4] Orsini. Accessed January 23, 2022. http://www.genmarenostrum.com/pagine-lettere/letterao/Orsini/orsini-gravina.htm.

Pignatelli
[1] "Pignatèlli Nell'enciclopedia Treccani." nell'Enciclopedia Treccani. Accessed January 4, 2022. http://www.treccani.it/enciclopedia/pignatelli/.

[2] "Pignatèlli, Ettore Nell'Enciclopedia Treccani." nell'Enciclopedia Treccani. Accessed January 4, 2022. http://www.treccani.it/enciclopedia/ettore-pignatelli.

[3] Pignatelli, Ferdinando I. Accessed January 4, 2022. https://clevergeek.imtqy.com/articles/6125911/.

[4] "Pignatèlli, Fabrizio Nell'enciclopedia Treccani." nell'Enciclopedia Treccani. Accessed January 4, 2022. http://www.treccani.it/enciclopedia/fabrizio-pignatelli.

Ruffo
14 "Ruffo Nell'enciclopedia Treccani." nell'Enciclopedia Treccani. Accessed January 4, 2022. http://www.treccani.it/enciclopedia/ruffo/.

15 "D'OPPIDO." Ruffo linee antiche. Accessed January 4, 2022. http://www.genmarenostrum.com/pagine-lettere/letterar/Ruffo/Ruffo%20linee%20antiche.htm.

[16] Ruffo di Bagnara E Castelcicala. Accessed January 4, 2022. http://www.genmarenostrum.com/pagine-lettere/letterar/Ruffo/Ruffo%20di%20bagnara.htm.

Saluzzo
[1] Wikipedia contributors, "Manfred I of Saluzzo," *Wikipedia, The Free Encyclopedia,* https://en.wikipedia.org/w/index.php?title=Manfred_I_of_Saluzzo&oldid=954350840 (accessed January 26, 2022).

[2] "Manfrédo II Marchese Di Saluzzo Nell'Enciclopedia Treccani." nell'Enciclopedia Treccani. Accessed December 23, 2021. http://www.treccani.it/enciclopedia/manfredo-ii-marchese-di-saluzzo.

[3] "Bonifacio Di Saluzzo." Wikipedia. Wikimedia Foundation, September 20, 2020. https://it.wikipedia.org/wiki/Bonifacio_di_Saluzzo.

[4] "Manfrédo III Marchese Di Saluzzo Nell'enciclopedia Treccani." nell'Enciclopedia Treccani. Accessed December 23, 2021. https://www.treccani.it/enciclopedia/manfredo-iii-marchese-di-saluzzo/.

[5] Wikipedia contributors, "Thomas I of Saluzzo," *Wikipedia, The Free Encyclopedia,* https://en.wikipedia.org/w/index.php?title=Thomas_I_of-Saluzzo&oldid=991260721 (accessed January 26, 2022).

[6] Wikipedia contributors, "Manfred IV of Saluzzo," *Wikipedia, The Free Encyclopedia,* https://en.wikipedia.org/w/index.php?title=Manfred_IV_of_Saluzzo&oldid=1061028592 (accessed January 26, 2022).

[7] Wikipedia contributors, "Thomas II of Saluzzo," *Wikipedia, The Free Encyclopedia,* https://en.wikipedia.org/w/index.php?title=Thomas_II_of_Saluzzo&oldid=954350988 (accessed January 26, 2022).

[8] Wikipedia contributors, "Thomas III of Saluzzo," *Wikipedia, The Free Encyclopedia,* https://en.wikipedia.org/w/index.php?title=Thomas_III_of_Saluzzo&oldid=1012789966 (accessed January 26, 2022).

[9] Famiglia Saluzzo. Accessed December 23, 2021. http://www.nobili-napoletani.it/Saluzzo.htm.

Sambiase
[1] Famiglia Sambiase. Accessed January 27, 2022. http://www.nobili-napoletani.it/Sambiase.htm.

[2] Sambiase. Accessed January 27, 2022. http://www.genmarenostrum.com/pagine-lettere/letteras/sambiase.htm.

Sanseverino

[1] Famiglia Sanseverino. Accessed January 27, 2022. http://www.nobili-napoletani.it/Sanseverino.htm.

[2] Sanseverino. Accessed January 27, 2022. http://www.genmarenos-trum.com/pagine-lettere/letteras/SANSEVERINO/SANSEVERINO2.htm.

Sforza

[1] "SFÒRZA, Muzio Attendolo Detto Lo Nell'Enciclopedia Treccani." nell'Enciclopedia Treccani. Accessed January 28, 2022. https://www.treccani.it/enciclopedia/muzio-attendolo-detto-lo-sforza/.

[2] "Sfòrza, Alessandro, Signore Di Pesaro Nell'enciclopedia Treccani." nell'Enciclopedia Treccani. Accessed January 28, 2022. https://www.treccani.it/enciclopedia/sforza-alessandro-signore-di-pesaro/.

Spinola

[1] Britannica, The Editors of Encyclopaedia. "Spinola Family". Encyclopedia Britannica, 20 Jul. 1998, https://www.britannica.com/topic/Spinola-family. Accessed 17 November 2021.

[2] Lecari, Andrea. "Spinola Doria, Paolo in 'Dizionario Biografico.'" in "Dizionario Biografico", 2018. http://www.treccani.it/enciclopedia/paolo-spinola-doria_%28Dizionario-Biografico%29/.

[3] Brunelli, Giampiero. "Spinola, Filippo in 'Dizionario Biografico.'" in "Dizionario Biografico", 2018. http://www.treccani.it/enciclopedia/filippo-spinola_%28Dizionario-Biografico%29/.

[4] Brunelli, Giampiero. "Spinola, Ambrogio in 'Dizionario Biografico.'" in "Dizionario Biografico", 2018. http://www.treccani.it/enciclopedia/ambrogio-spinola_%28Dizionario-Biografico%29/.

Spinelli

[1] Famiglia Spinelli, accessed December 17, 2021, http://www.nobili-napoletani.it/Spinelli.htm.

[2] "INDEX OF NOBLE FAMILIES OF THE MEDITERRANEAN." Indice Spinelli. Accessed December 17, 2021. http://www.genmarenostrum.com/pagine-lettere/letteras/spinelli/spinelli1.htm.

Visconti

[1] Britannica, The Editors of Encyclopaedia. "Visconti Family". Encyclopedia Britannica, 14 Jun. 2002, https://www.britannica.com/topic/Visconti-family. Accessed 20 November 2021.

[2] Grillo, Paolo. "Visconti, Matteo in 'Dizionario Biografico.'" in "Dizionario Biografico", 2020. http://www.treccani.it/enciclopedia/matteo-visconti_%28Dizionario-Biografico%29/.

[3] "Stefano Visconti." Wikipedia. Wikimedia Foundation, October 3, 2021. https://en.wikipedia.org/wiki/Stefano_Visconti.

[4] "Galeazzo I Visconti." Wikipedia. Wikimedia Foundation, August 7, 2021. https://en.wikipedia.org/wiki/Galeazzo_I_Visconti.

[5] "Bernabò Visconti." Military Wiki. Accessed December 22, 2021. https://military-history.fandom.com/wiki/Bernab%C3%B2_Visconti.

Nobiliary Titles

[17] regalis.com/nobletitles.htmMendola, Louis. "Italian Titles of Nobility." Italian titles of nobility - a concise, Accurate Guide to nobiliary history, tradition and law in Italy until 1946 - facts, not fiction., 2015. http://regalis.com/nobletitles.htm.

[18] Mendola, Louis. "Italian Titles of Nobility." Italian titles of nobility - a concise, Accurate Guide to nobiliary history, tradition and law in Italy until 1946 - facts, not fiction., 2015. http://regalis.com/nobletitles.htm.

About the Author

Robert was born in Whitestone NY and grew up in College Point. During his childhood he spent a great deal of time at his maternal grandmother's house in Corona. Both of his parents' families had strong Italian roots and followed traditions from Italy. After retiring from banking in 2014, he began to dedicate his time to finding his roots in earnest. In 2018 he started a blog, and the fol-lowing year a podcast, both to promote the research of Italian ancestry.

© Italian Market Place LLC

Lori, Me, John and Mom